Discover Charleston West Virginia

History – Culture - Entertainment

First Printing: October 2007

ISBN 10: 1-933817-32-1
ISBN 13: 978-1-933817-32-3

Printed in the USA by
Profits Publishing of Sarasota, Florida
http://profitspublishing.com

Table of Contents

Chapter 1

Introduction

There are many reasons why Charleston, West Virginia is an outstanding city. It's an area rich in history, well rooted in the forming of our nation. It is a part of the only state formed directly by the Civil War, and it's one of only two states that was formed through seceding from another (the other state that was formed this way is Vermont). As the capitol city of West Virginia, Charleston manages to be both on the cutting edge of political decision-making and a city of small-town charm.

Charleston has much to offer, including numerous cultural activities, entertainment, education, superior medical care, and just plain fun. Whether your taste runs to the postcard-worthy beautiful architecture, or breathtaking views of the wide, meandering Kanawha River and the rugged mountains beyond it, Charleston has something for you.

See the beauty of nature as well as the art of man. Watch the heart of industry as barges transport coal up and down the river daily. Hear the music of the 70-year-old Symphony Orchestra, the Mountain Stage Band, or enjoy one of the many local music venues. Smell the mouth-watering delights at the Capitol Market, an open-air-style market inside the train depot. Sample the menu at one of the mainstay restaurants, like Joe Fazio's (it's been around since 1934) or seek out something trendy, like Sushi Atlantic on Shrewsbury Street.

While state government often dictates the atmosphere of the business environment, Charleston is a city that has abundant natural resources all around; so the city has always worked to maintain its own vitality through both the public and private sectors. As a result, economic challenges have been minimal, and the city's future is strong.

Although the river valley is a fertile area, where crops like tobacco, corn, hay, and fruits can grow, there is not as much farming as one might expect. Instead, West Virginia is one of the leaders in producing bituminous coal; the state also produces natural gas, salt, oil, and stone.

Technology is a leading source of industry in the Kanawha River valley. Glass and chemical plants utilize some of the area's natural resources. There are also manufacturers of metal and machinery.

A river town, if you've never lived in one, is an ideal place for raising a family. Charleston offers every amenity: swimming pools, tennis courts, baseball fields, a minor-league baseball team. There are plays, musicals, storytelling, and concerts. Festivals celebrate the arts, and the Vandalia Gathering every Memorial Day celebrates the traditions of the area. The Sternwheel Regatta on Labor Day offers a chance to learn about the river boats, take in local cuisine, or even take a ride on a Sternwheeler. National acts entertain each evening, while everyone can participate in the AARP Power Walk, the Charleston Distance Run, and the Grand Feature Parade.

A reporter for the Gallipolis (Ohio) Dispatch had this to say about the city in 1861: "Charleston is quite a pretty place. It is located on the beautiful bottom on the northeast bank of the river and is entirely surrounded by lofty hills. There are many pretty residences but they and the public buildings are built after the old style and have not much pretension to magnificence."

One thing Charleston is not is a copy of a well-known historical southern city. A settlement was actually started here in 1788, and the city was named for one of its forbears.

Visitors here inevitably are drawn to the gold-domed capitol building that glistens above the skyline; but soon they see the vast array of entertainment and recreation, and their attention is diverted.

The Capitol Complex is a good starting point for a visit, though; the city's fascinating past and the state's rich history give even the casual visitor an instant fascination about this "wild and wonderful" place. Outdoors, you almost instantly notice the monuments that are beautifully displayed on the park-like grounds.

Charleston's Cultural Center at the Capitol Complex is home to the Commission on the Arts, the State Historic Preservation Office, the State Museum, State Archives, and more. The Cultural Center opened in 1976 and showcases the artistic, cultural, and historical heritage of the state. Here you can browse through the State Archives library, the photographic collection, or visit one of the numerous events and lectures that are held throughout the year. You can search for your family's genealogy or simply learn about history.

The Cultural Center is open Monday through Thursday 9 a.m. to 8 p.m., Friday and Saturday 9 a.m. to 6 p.m. and Sunday Noon to 6 p.m. The Cultural Center offices are open Monday through Friday from 8:30am to 5pm. The Cultural Center is located in the Capitol Complex at 1900 Kanawha Boulevard East. For more information, please phone (304) 558-0220.

After noticing the initial beauty and charm, most visitors comment on the friendliness and hospitality of the residents. It's hard to understand how a bustling capital city can be so welcoming—but that's what happens in Charleston!

Facts about Charleston

- Charleston, is the largest city and the capital city of West Virginia
- The population is about 51,300.
- Charleston's metropolitan population is more than 250,000.

- Charleston is situated at the intersection of three major interstates: I-64, I-77, and I-79.
- The average high temperature is about 77 degrees. The average low is 34 degrees.
- State Bird: Cardinal
- State Flower: Rhododendron
- State Motto: Montani semper liberi—Mountaineers are always free
- State Nickname: Mountain State
- State Song: The West Virginia Hills

Chapter 2

The River: Bringing People And Commerce

The Kanawha River (kə-nô'wə) is formed at the junction of New River and Gauley River above Kanawha Falls, about 30 miles from Charleston. In fact, Native American tribes identified the New River and The Kanawha River as one. Thomas Jefferson, in his Notes on the State of Virginia (1781) referred to it as a single river called "the Great Kanhaway".

Jefferson wrote:

> "The Great Kanhaway is a river of considerable note for the fertility of its lands, and still more as leading towards the headwaters of James River. Nevertheless, it is doubtful whether its great and numerous rapids will admit a navigation, but at an expence to which it will require ages to render its inhabitants equal. The great obstacles begin at what are called the Great Falls, 90 miles above the mouth, below which are only five or six rapids, and these passable, with some difficulty, even at low water."

The year was 1819. The steamboat Robert Thompson was sent down the Kanawha River in order to see whether it was possible to navigate all the way to

Charleston. The rapids proved too difficult to pass, even after two days' effort; the boat returned to the Ohio River. As a result, the Virginia Assembly made an appropriation to improve the river so that in 1820 the *Albert Donnally* did reach Charleston.

The river was enhanced so that three feet of water could be secured to the Kanawha Falls all year. The improvements were created through a series of sluices and wing dams. Those who traveled were at the mercy of water levels that fluctuated wildly, as well as boulders and other snags that were in the water at low levels. These were removed by 1840 so that the river could handle traffic of coal, salt and timber. The locks and dams controlled the depths – more were built in future years to control the waters which often flooded the lower lying communities.

The loads of coal grew larger over the years. By the 1850's many shipments of coal were being sent downriver, creating a need for even more improvements on the sluice and wing dam system.

The Civil War interrupted the work on the river; however, steamships known as packets were able to run daily between Charleston and Gallipolis carrying passengers, freight, and mail. This service continued until the war was over.

The Civil War was clearly a critical event in history for the United States, but perhaps more so for Virginia than any other state. After ongoing differences between Eastern and Western Virginia, in 1893 Virginia was severed and West Virginia was formed. President Lincoln grudgingly went along with the plan, although he is said to have felt that the statehood bill was forced on him.

At that time the State took over the Kanawha River, creating a board to collect tolls and make improvements. In 1870 Congress decided that work would proceed on the locks and dams, A few years later the Kanawha Board undertook the improvements, but soon found it to be too much and transferred all the rights to the Kanawha River to the United States government in 1875. The U.S. Government undertook the project of providing a navigable depth of six feet year around throughout all 96 miles of the river. This project, though challenging, proved to be a huge factor in the industrialization of West Virginia. By 1904 they had spent $4,271,863 and there were 1,406,484 tons of freight per year being carried via river.

The Name of the River

Where the Kanawha River got its name remains a mystery; there are endless myths about the origins. Most people agree that it's derived from an Indian word but—from which tribal language?

Was it named for an Indian tribe that lived along the river in the 1700s? Or possibly the Piscataway Indians, who lived on Conoy Island, (Kanaw) a short form of Kanawha? And the Miamis called it "Piquemetami," which doesn't sound anything at all like Kanawha.

Captain Pierre-Joseph Celeron called the Kanawha River "Chinodaista" in the mid 1700s. He traveled with a number of French Mohawks, so it is thought that this was a Mohawk word.

Some say that the name Great Kanawha is derived from the word Kenininsheka, "river of the evil spirits" (from the Shawnee language).

Some say it means "place of the white stone", from the Delaware tribe; the reference to white stone undoubtedly means the salt deposits that once were so plentiful.

Regardless of what its name means, the river has provided a great source of industry through coal, natural gas, and transportation for the area throughout history. It is West Virginia's largest waterway, meandering for 43 miles through Kanawha County in a northwest direction to its mouth at the Ohio River in Point Pleasant. Today it intertwines along with Interstate 64, which crosses the Kanawha in four places.

Salt Furnaces

Salt making important; many of the springs and creeks were "deer licks"; Mrs. Mary ingles made salt at Malden in 1755 while a captive of Indians. Dickinson salt works at Malden was in continuous use for 90 years (still 1923 talking). The flow of brine is as strong today as ever; average depth of wells 850 feet. Barges floated salt down Kanawha, Ohio, and MS rivers to market. Sold at Memphis, Louisville, Paducah, and Nashville;

boatmen sold the salt barge and all and found there way home. At one time there were over 60 salt furnaces along the Kanawha River within 10 miles of the city of Charleston.

Salt was the first mineral to be developed as an Industry in West Virginia. In fact, the salt springs were known and used by the Indians as far back as the late 1700s. Mary Draper Ingles, a pioneer captured by a Shawnee raiding party, was forced to make salt by her Indian captors in 1755 while other Indians hunted game. She did this by boiling brine in a kettle. (For the full story of Mary's capture and her daring escape, see chapter 3)

The area where Mary was taken as a captive was called the "Great Buffalo Lick." It was on the north side of the river, near the mouth of Campbell's Creek. Today the town of Malden is located there. It was directly across the river from where Daniel Boone resided in 1790-1791. Hundreds of bison, elk, and other animals visited the lick during Boone's time.

In 1774, Andrew Lewis' army fought Indians here on their way to the Battle of Point Pleasant. When the pioneers won the battle, they began settling the Kanawha valley and taking advantage of the salt springs.

In the year 1797 Elisha Brooks set up the first furnace in the area for commercially manufacturing salt. He was able to sell all that he could produce; soon the banks of the river were lined with salt furnaces. A village grew up there where lead, gun powder etc were sold; settlers came from far away in all directions to obtain salt, which they carried back on horseback or by flat boat, or even canoe, on the river. The salt provided these European-American pioneers with a way to cure butter and meat.

Salt from the Kanawha area was red, due to the way that Elisha Brooks and his successors manufactured it. The brine was boiled down in a series of small kettles that sat over a chimney flue. The boiling process oxidizes the carbonate of iron that exists in the brine; this oxidation causes the reddish tint. Brooks produced upwards of 150 pounds of salt a day selling it for 8 to 10 cents per pound.

In 1806 David and Joseph Ruffner decided to dig a deep well to manufacture salt on the commercial level. Their deep well drill was probably the first in America. In fact, the deep well drilling the Ruffner brothers did was so well known that when Titusville, Pennsylvania businessmen decided to drill America's first oil well, the Ruffner salt works drillers were called in to do the work. The Ruffners also used local coal for furnace fuel, so they were able to undercut earlier prices through their large supply of brine and the low cost of fuel.

By 1835 there were 40 salt furnaces in operation in the Kanawha Saltines, which is the area from just above present day Charleston 12 to 15 miles upriver along both sides of the river. This contained the villages now known as Malden and Browntown.

The salt furnaces produced 2,000,000 bushels of salt per year. These had a market value of 50 cents per bushel.

Because there was a blockade by the British navy during the War of 1812, salt couldn't be transported from other sources safely. At one time there were 300 flatboats in service at once, hauling salt down the river. So the industry in the Valley was suddenly booming. The Kanawha Salines had nearly a two decade monopoly on salt production throughout most of the country. In fact, the Kanawha Valley salt manufacturers banded together and formed what is often referred to as the nation's first trust, the Kanawha Salt Company. They agreed to combine and also reduce their production in order to raise salt prices in the west.

This early salt industry went into a sharp decline by the end of the century, largely due to railway expansion; but it opened the way for the chemical industry to develop in the Kanawha Valley soon after. Also while drilling for salt, Captain James Wilson struck the first natural gas well in 1815. It was drilled near the present-day state capitol complex, near Brooks Street and Kanawha Boulevard. As the area's mountains were stripped of timber used to fire the salt furnaces, David Ruffner substituted coal instead; thus, he began the industrial use of coal.

Marmet is the name of the city that began as Elizaville in 1773. It was later named Browntown, for salt magnate Charles Brown. The name was changed again after 1899 when the Marmet Coal Company began developing much of the land in the area.

If you go there...

Malden, just outside Charleston on Rt. 60, is part of the Midland Trail Scenic Highway. With only about 800 residents, it carries remnants of its history proudly. Tour the Salt Village that contains the Booker T. Washington cabin replica and the African Zion Baptist Church, where Washington taught. For tours, make an appointment through Cabin Creek Quilts.

Self-guided heritage tours of the town make you feel like a part of the past. The Hale, Norton, and Putney Houses are located on Malden Drive, and Welch-Oakes is toward the river on Fallam Drive.

The Putney House, built in 1836, is used as a law office. The Welch-Oakes House, built about 1843, is used as a private residence.

The African Zion Baptist Church was started in 1850 and was West Virginia's first black Baptist Church. Booker T. Washington attended services there, and taught there after his college graduation in 1875. The church meets now in a frame building that was created around 1872; it is listed on the Historical Register.

Kanawha Salines Presbyterian Church is still in use and is the oldest church in Malden. The church was organized in 1819 by the Ruffners; the brick building was constructed in 1840. Just behind the church is the former home of Minnie Wayne Cooper (1907-1989). She was a local leader and teacher, and a friend of the Washington family.

The old Dickenson home is still in use by one of its heirs; the TerraSalis Garden Center is in the northeast corner of the property, featuring four acres of display gardens as well as a full service garden center. The remains of the family's salt works is fenced in on the grounds as well.

Visit Malden via I-64 exit 96 Midland Trail (Route 60 East). Take the Malden exit. Turn left at the stop sign and drive about one mile.

The Great Flood

Near the beginning of the Civil war, the Great Flood destroyed most of the salt works in 47 different locations along the riverbanks. Water rose to its highest known level. Many salt entrepreneurs lost their fortunes. Most of them remained in decline; somehow, between the flood and the war, the business never bounced back as one would expect.

The flood occurred on Sept 29, 1861. It is referred to as the Great Kanawha River Flood of Record; it also flooded nearby tributaries like the Elk River.

It is said that the river in Charleston rose three to four feet, peaking at over 46 feet. This flooding and the subsequent discharged caused the Ohio River to flow upstream for 30 miles.

The Civil War in West Virginia

Western and Eastern Virginia had political differences even before the start of the Civil War. There were also social and economic differences. The westerners were hard-working families who owned few slaves; easterners utilized slave labor and had plenty of leisure time.

The westerners felt that they weren't represented fairly in the government because the Constitution allowed each county to have two representatives, so the eastern portion of the state was more heavily represented. There were in fact 360,000 white people in Western Virginia compared with 16,000 slaves. Voting was allowed according to how much land a person owned, so the 8% of the population who were able to vote were mainly from eastern Virginia. Voting rights were granted only to white males who owned at least 25 acres of improved land or 50 acres of unimproved land; this was bad news to many western Virginians, who for the most part didn't own the land they lived on. The constitution also gave two delegates per county to represent them in the General Assembly, which gave eastern Virginia better leverage.

There were even religious differences between the two sides of the state: the eastern counties practiced Protestant religions, while the west was inhabited largely by European immigrants. These immigrants might also be part of Quaker, Mennonite, and Dunkard religions, which had no history of slavery. In general, though, they were opposed to it.

In 1830, a new constitution was just barely approved which didn't meet any of the western inhabitants' demands for better representation and direct election of officials. Immediately, the cry went out for secession.

Western Virginia, which would later become the state of West Virginia, was important to the new Confederacy, in part because the tough farm boys there were expected to volunteer for the army and in part because the Kanawha Valley produced something that was lacking throughout most of the South: Salt. Salt was necessary for the preservation of food—so it was a must-have, not a luxury flavoring as we think of it today.

In 1859, John Brown and his followers raided the United States Armory and Arsenal at Harpers Ferry. They were forced to withdraw into an engine house; surviving members of his group were captured there on October 18. Brown was hanged on December 2nd. While Southerners were angered by his attempts to establish a colony for runaway slaves, many in the North supported his actions and mourned him as a martyr.

The battle over slavery was now at a fevered pitch. As the question of statehood for Western Virginia (alternately called "Kanawha" and "New Virginia") came into play, the slavery issue hung like a pall over the convention members. One idea that was taken into consideration was a gradual emancipation. Another was that new slaves should be forbidden to enter the state. The final document said, "No slave shall be brought, or free person of color be permitted to come into this state for permanent residence."

All of these factors played a part in the division between the two sides in the Civil War. Soldiers' loyalties lay on one or another depending on their family, location, and circumstance—sometimes causing a confusing, heartbreaking internal battle. During the Civil War West Virginia contributed about 32,000 soldiers to the Union Army—and at the same time about 10,000 to the Confederate side.

Western Virginia was a split state during the Civil War, contributing over 30,000 soldiers to the Union side and around 10,000 to the Confederates. By June of 1861, Captain Patton's' Kanawha Riflemen had joined forces with Captain Swann's company and two others, led by Colonel Christopher Tompkins. The Charleston Company had begun in 1856 as the Kanawha Minutemen, changing their name in 1859 to the Kanawha Riflemen. Composed of elite members of Charleston's society, this Company had the reputation as the best-drilled formation in the Confederate Army—largely due to their leader, Captain Patton.

In 1861, the First Kanawha Regiment was comprised of companies from several counties:

Company A	Border Riflemen	Putnam County
Company C	Mountain Cove Guards	Fayette County
Company D	Nicholas Blues	Nicholas County
Company E	Elk River Tigers	Clay County
Company F	Rocky Point Greys	Monroe County
Company G	Wyoming Riflemen	Wyoming County
Company H	Kanawha Riflemen	Kanawha County
Company I	Boone Company	Fayette County
Company J	Kanawha Rangers	Boone County
Company K	Fayetteville Rifles	Fayette County[1]

The men felt a great deal of internal conflict during the creation of the company. The Kanawha Riflemen sent a statement to the government making it clear that they didn't want to raise arms against Virginia or other Southern states. They were located far from the

[1]Husley, Val: "Men of Virginia – Men of Kanawha – To Arms", West Virginia History, Vol. XXXV, No. 3, page 222.

Confederate supply bases, connected only by roads that would be impassable should the weather fail.

Recruits for the Confederates were required to furnish their own uniforms, which were amateur at best, often sporting the wrong decoration for the soldier's military rank, or identifying them as cavalry instead of infantry. All sorts of weapons were seen in the First and Second Kanawha Volunteer Regiments, including squirrel guns, pistols, and flintlocks.

Battle of Scary Creek

This skirmish took place on July 17, 1861 between Confederates, which were led by Captain George Patton, and Federals who were under General Jacob Cox. Patton was wounded at Scary Creek, so Captain Albert Jenkins, a lawyer who was educated at Harvard, took over. Jenkins' actions led to the victory, the first for Southerners in an open fight. Technically the Confederates won the battle, but Colonel Patton was wounded and some of the Virginians panicked. General Henry Wise decided to retreat to Sewell Mountain, where General Lee was stationed—so the area was left in Federal Hands. The battle took 20 Federal lives and five Confederate ones. The Union soldiers' graves were found near U.S. 35 in the 1920s.

One soldier's name who fought at Scary Creek became more famous than that of any other: "Devil Anse" Hatfield, leader of the legendary clan that feuded with the McCoys. You can read more about the Hatfields and McCoys near the end of Chapter 4.

After the Battle of Scary Creek, Jenkins was made a Colonel of the Eighth Virginia Regiment. His original troops, the Border Rangers, became Company E.7.

The former Virginia Governor, now General Henry Wise and his men were driven back by Northern troops led by Jacob Cox. Cox's men drove Wise to Gauley Bridge and back toward Greenbrier County. But in August, as they marched toward Gauley Bridge, General Rosecrans' forces were defeated. Union troops attacked General John Floyd on September 10, driving Floyd and his political rival Wise both back to Greenbrier County. This battle served to place the Kanawha Valley in Union hands early on during the war. This was especially significant because, with their early victories in both the Kanawha and Monongahela Valleys, the Union held control of the Baltimore and Ohio Railroad throughout the remainder of the war.

On April 17, the Virginia state convention had voted to secede from the Union. Within a few weeks, delegates from 25 counties met at the First Wheeling Convention in order to discuss the secession; they did not accept it. The debate dragged on for months, and at one point voters wanted to create a new state called Kanawha. By late November, despite the opposition from many voters, the state was to be called West Virginia; its boundaries were extended and a constitution drawn up.

On December 3, 1861, the name of the new state was up for debate. Many names were suggested, debated, and voted on or discarded. The names and votes that were eventually counted turned out as follows:

West Virginia - 30.

Kanawha -9.

Western Virginia - 2.

Allegheny- 2.

Augusta - 1.

So it was that the new state was called West Virginia.

1862: The Battle of Charleston

During the summer of 1862, the Secretary of War wired to General William W. Loring an order to clear the Valley of the Kanawha, and operate northwardly to a junction with the army in the valley. Loring dispatched Albert G. Jenkins on a raid above New River, and on September 6 he began a march down the south side of the river with about 5,000 men. Confederate and Union forces met on September 10 near Fayetteville, battling all day.

The Federal Regiments were under command of Colonel Joseph Andrew Jackson Lightburn, a good friend of Stonewall Jackson. Lightburn was concerned about the approach of Loring's Confederate troops, but he also had to consider the northern threat created by Albert Jenkins and the Confederate Cavalry.

On September 11, the Federals split forces near Gauley's Bridge, with the enemy troops in pursuit. Gauley

Bridge, which had been burned by Wise during the previous summer, had been spectacularly rebuilt. It was constructed in twenty-three working days and was considered a modern marvel. Five hundred eighty-five feet long, ten feet wide, and "ingeniously braced", it was said to be so thoroughly trussed that a cavalry riding over it wouldn't produce a vibration.

The Federals got behind the Union forces, strengthening their positions on either side of the road to Gauley Bridge. By sunset, fighting slowed; when the Federals heard of the arrival of General Echols' Confederate brigade, they withdrew and retreated to Gauley Bridge.

On the 11th during the retreat, the bridge at the Town of Gauley Bridge was destroyed. There seemed to be much question about how it was destroyed; local residents said that Federal troops tried to burn it, but that the timbers were still too green to ignite. So instead, the cables were hacked with axes.

The *Republican,* a newspaper in Middleport, Ohio, reported this in 1915:

"This order was issued by Lieutenant Colonel Dayton, of the Federal Forces, to first duty sergeant Donald McDonald, a member of Company A 4th West Virginia Infantry. "Sergeant McDonald, detail twelve men, and go back and burn Gauley Bridge after our wagon train from Fayetteville has passed over it.""

"The Federal wagon train rumbled across and then McDonald and his twelve men applied the torch...but he was too late to make an escape with his men.

McDonald and his men fled up the side of the steep mountain to the northward, and hid in the thick woods until the next morning when the attempted to find their way out."

Early on the morning of the 13th, a Federal brigade crossed the Elk River and took up defensive positions along the shore near Charleston. A small battle took place near the present location of the state's capitol building. The attackers were the 22nd Virginia from the Kanawha Valley. The exiles, George Patton's Kanawha Riflemen, were home again.

The Federals began to attempt to defend the west bank of the Elk River at its mouth into the Kanawha. This was a great defensive position; the Federal wagon train carrying large amounts of war supplies had a way to escape toward the Ohio River. The 9th West Virginia infantry regiment moved into position along the Elk River, putting up log breastworks for protection. The 34th Ohio crossed the Elk on a suspension Bridge and prepared to receive an attack. The 4th West Virginia Infantry, freshly evacuated from Fayetteville, came in to assist.

The Kanawha hotel, the Bank, the Southern Methodist Church, a warehouse, and the Mercer Academy were burned. Federal forces set fire to the bridge and then cut the cables. They held the Confederates in check with cannon fire just long enough to let their army retreat.

Charleston residents were terrified by rumors that were flying throughout the city. They alternately heard that it was going to be burned from one side to the other, then that it was to be shelled. Residents evacuated to the cemetery on Cox's Hill, only to find they were in greater danger there because the Confederates were positioned higher on the hill firing on retreating Union soldiers. They hoisted a white flag made from a lady's undergarment, attaching it to the top of a martin nesting box. Other residents decided to leave town and commandeered boats, canoes, rafts, and anything else they could find.

The river was said to be literally covered with flat boats, jerry boats, jolly boats, skiffs, and more. From daylight throughout the day, a person could have almost crossed the river simply by stepping from one boat to the next. The fighting became more intense when the Confederates shelled the Federal positions across the Elk River. About 3 p.m. Lightburn found himself outnumbered by about two to one, hampered by his 700 wagon loads of supplies. Lightburn retreated from the Valley, moving his troops over one hundred miles and saving about a million dollars in supplies from capture by Loring's regiments. He reported his loss as 25 killed, 95 wounded and 190 missing. Loring moved in to rescue the people from the "counterfeit state government."

The Confederates had forced the Union out of the Kanawha Valley. More importantly, the South now had control of the salt works.

Only six weeks later, though, the Union regained control of the city, remaining there until the end of the war.

The Union managed to drive the Confederates out of the Monongahela and Kanawha Valleys, and controlled the B&O railroad throughout the rest of the war.

If you go there...

The West Virginia Museum of History, housed in the Cultural Center at the capitol complex, displays many items from the history of the formation of the state of West Virginia.

If you take I-64 West and take exit 58-A, then bear right on Oakwood Avenue and right on Fort Hill Drive, you'll find the neighborhood that once was Fort Scammon, the union fortification. In September 1862, before it was a fort, the Confederates used the area as an artillery position.

The Hurricane Bridge is only a few miles away (see story following). Continue on I-64 west to exit 34 and turn right on U.S. 60 to get there.

If you get back on I-64 and take exit 11, drive toward Huntington, turn right on Ninth Avenue, right on 20th street, and veer left onto Norway Avenue, you will find the Spring Hill Cemetery. If you take the second entrance, the confederate burial ground will be on your right. This is where General Jenkins' grave is located, just behind the Confederate Monument. Jenkins led the first invasion of the North in 1862.

1863: Hurricane Bridge

During 1863, the North continued to hold onto western Virginia, despite several raids. On March 28, 1863, a force under Jenkins (the Harvard-trained lawyer who led at the Battle of Scary Creek after Patton's injury) attacked Union troops under Captain Johnson, a few hundred yards right of the bridge. Jenkins rather arrogantly sent a message to Captain Johnson saying that the

Confederates had many more troops and that Johnson should surrender. Johnson refused to do so, suspecting it could be a ruse. "I'll not do so unless forced to do so by an exhibition of your boasted strength," he replied.

The fight lasted many hours; each side only lost a few men. Interestingly, Jenkins fell back, although he could easily have forced a surrender. He was later criticized for doing so. His troops outnumbered those of Johnson by 4 to one; his suggestion that Johnson drop back had been no idle threat.

Jenkins, however, was not a soldier, but an Ivy League lawyer; so perhaps his poor decisions were not entirely his fault. He was neither a trained nor skilled military man. In fact, before the war he was a well-known attorney and was voted into the House of Representatives in 1857. He resigned that post in 1861.

At any rate, twelve days later he surprised the men at Point Pleasant, driving them into the courthouse for protection. However, he and his men did not have troops or equipment to drive the men out of the courthouse. Eventually he took his men and crossed the Kanawha River.

On May 18, Confederate General John McCausland attacked White's forces in hopes of defeating them and moving on the coveted Kanawha Valley salt mines. White's forces consisted of the Twelfth Regiment Ohio Volunteer Infantry, two companies of the Second West Virginia Cavalry, and two sections of Captain J.R.

McMullin's battery. He was later reinforced by three infantry regiments.

Colonel Jonathan D. Hines, commanding the Twelfth Ohio, sent a force of four companies under Captain Robert Wilson to repel McCausland's troops on the Raleigh Road. Wilson's men waited at Blake's Farm, seven miles from Fayetteville. During the night, McCausland circled around Wilson and the next morning began firing on him from both sides. Wilson was forced to retreat back to camp. McCausland followed and opened artillery fire, which he kept up until dark.

McMullin's battery returned the fire, but McCausland was shielded by timber and underbrush. He was safe from the counterattack.

Very early the next morning, the enemy's artillery began shelling the position held by the Thirteenth, and the regiment was under their fire until about 1:30 P.M. This was the very first indirect artillery fire (action taken against an unseen target) in military history. The action was taken by a 19-year-old Confederate, Sgt. Milton Humphreys. The enemy retreated and the Thirteenth was part of the brigade sent in pursuit.

The next morning shots were exchanged; McCausland's forces again retreated, and the pursuing troops followed for approximately 10 miles.

The next morning, Companies B, F, and G of the Thirteenth, under Lieutenant Colonel James R. Hall, were sent into the town as skirmishers, but found it evacuated. Later that day, the regiment was ordered to return to camp at Fayetteville, where it arrived on the morning of May 23. They were unable to make headway at Fayetteville. Several of the companies were transferred back and forth until July from Cotton Hill to Hurricane Bridge and back to Camp White.

More about General Jenkins

Albert Gallatin Jenkins was born on a plantation at Greenbottom. He attended college at the age of fourteen and went on to attend Harvard University Law School; he was admitted to the bar by age 20. He was a delegate to the National Democratic Convention, but in 1861 he resigned his Congressional seat.

In addition to leading in battles at Scary Creek and Hurricane Bridge, Jenkins led the first invasion of the North in 1862, a short thrust across the Ohio River. This was considered his most brilliant military exploit. Although burning property was common during raids, Jenkins assured the Ohio residents that he would not burn there property. Along with 550 cavalry troops, he swept through, destroyed the Baltimore and Ohio railroad, and returned to the Kanawha Valley to take the enemy from the rear.

While serving as a soldier, Jenkins was elected to represent the Fourteenth Virginia Congressional District in the first Congress of Confederate States. He served from the date that it opened, February 18, 1862, until August 6 of that year when he was given the commission of brigadier general, and was sent back to battle.

In June 1863, Jenkins cooperated with General R.E. Rodes to perform simultaneous attacks on Winchester and Berryville, in the Shenandoah Valley. They also immediately attacked Martinsburg, then moved into Maryland. The fall of Martinsburg was a pivotal event in clearing the U.S. forces from the Shenandoah Valley. Jenkins' men then obtained horses, which were supposed to be purchased through normal channels; but Jenkins didn't ask his men to account for their unusually large number of horses.

Jenkins also led one of the first occupations in Pennsylvania (Chambersburg, 1863) ten days before the Battle of Gettysburg. He made his residence at the home of the editor of the Repository. He withdrew his troops temporarily, which unfortunately allowed his supplies to be taken. However he and his men returned and moved forward to assist Rodes in his attacks on Harrisonburg.

By 1864, Jenkins was appointed Commander of the Department of Western Virginia. His headquarters were located at Dublin. When Brigadier General George Crook, leading the Second Infantry Division of the Department of West Virginia, learned that Jenkins was at Dublin he took a vast number of troops on an expedition there.

General Jenkins was injured at Dublin, commonly referred to as Cloyd's Mountain in 1864, requiring that his arm be amputated. Sick with pneumonia already, it is said that an orderly passing by knocked the ligature (a tool used to stop the flow of blood from his arm) off his stump and he bled to death. Jenkins' body was brought to rest in Spring Hill Cemetery near Huntington in 1861.

During this period, Western Virginia soldiers also played significant roles on other fronts; members of the 4th West Virginia Infantry played a role in the siege of Vicksburg, Mississippi.

The Civil War was referred to as a war of brother against brother and father against son; certainly no state serves as a better example of this description than the state of West Virginia, where support for the northern and southern causes was nearly equal. Many families were split down the middle because of their beliefs on the war. There were many instances of divided loyalties, and even of individuals fighting for both sides. During the Battle of Scary Creek, it is said that a Confederate soldier supposedly saw his brothers fighting on the other battle lines and changed sides on the spot.

The divisions caused by the Civil War lasted long after the war ended, usually acted out in political venues and occasionally developing into violence. Military service in the Civil War was a badge of honor for both Union and Confederate veterans. The Battle of Gettysburg reunion, another symbol of the division the Civil War created, saw about the same number of Union and Confederate veterans from West Virginia.

Altogether, West Virginia saw 632 battles or skirmishes throughout the duration of the Civil War.

Inside the Cultural Center just across from the Capitol, the West Virginia Museum of History is housed. The basement of the museum holds the first Confederate flag that was captured in battle. A large flag, too big for carrying in battle, it must have been flying from a staff. It was captured on June 3, 1861. It looks as if it was cut and resewn from a United States flag. It was not an official flag, because it depicts 15 stars rather than the seven stars in a circle that were the official emblem of the flag. These represented the first seven states to secede from the Union. The Confederacy had 11 charter states, plus two unofficial states (Maryland and Kentucky). So it seems that 11 or 13 stars would have made more sense. The flag maker might have thought Missouri would join, but unfortunately he left us no clue as to why there were 15 stars on this flag.

Since the U.S. Constitution clearly stated that no state can be created from another without the original state's legislature consent, there was a question about the legality of creating West Virginia from Virginia. The museum contains a display about this occurrence. The Virginia legislature (located in Confederate Richmond) had no intention of agreeing to the split, and President Lincoln's cabinet was divided over the issue. Lincoln somehow managed to split hairs, stating that there was a difference between "secession against the Constitution and in favor of the Constitution." He sent the vote to be decided by the Union loyalists who had created a "legislature" in Wheeling—the ones who had brought up the idea in the first place. They immediately approved statehood, and West Virginia was admitted to the Union in June, 1863.

The 1870s: a series of firsts

The 1870s brought about many changes in Charleston. The first gas lights went into the downtown area. Dr. John Hale, a descendent of Mary Ingles, was Mayor of Charleston. He paved the first brick street at his own expense. He built the first theatre and began the first public delivery of ice. He also established the area's first steam laundry and the first wholesale grocery. The first steam ferries were his doing also—and his own steamboats were named "Lame Duck" and "Wild Goose."

The area's first "skyscraper"—three stories tall—was built in 1872 on the waterfront by J.M. Gates. Gates Paint Manufacturing sold wholesale paints, roofing, etc. Front Street or Water Street originally housed all the businesses, which at that time were wholesale businesses.

If you're looking for ways to enjoy the river...

Consider the Kanawha State Forest, only 20 minutes from downtown Charleston. Also within an easy drive are Beech Fork State Park, East Lynn Lake, and many other favored hunting and fishing spots. Between Point Pleasant and Huntington you'll find the Green Bottom Wildlife Management Area.

Coonskin Park is a picturesque facility with a boathouse, clubhouse, tennis courts, putt putt and par 3 golf, and a swimming pool. Open daily except Christmas Day, you can reach Coonskin Park off the Greenbrier Street exit north of Charleston; drive about 5 miles on State Route 114.

A new century

New industries continued to develop in Charleston as the city became the center for state government. Coal, gas, and the railroad expansion, as well as chemical, glass timber and steel brought much construction to the area.

After the Civil War, chemical plants began developing in the valley producing bromide. Both Warner-Klipstein and Rollins Chemical established themselves to produce chlorine, barium peroxide, barium salts. Later the Pickering Chemical Company and The Roessler and Hasslacher Chemical Company (at St. Albans) began production. Numerous other names came and went, including Union Carbide Corporation and the Clendenin Gasoline Company.

During World War II, Charleston's Institute proved to be the largest synthetic rubber producer in the U.S., making over half the rubber needed for the war effort. The chemical plants continue to give to the economy today what the demise of the coal industry took away.

To learn more about the history of Charleston and its industry....

Visit the South Charleston Museum, located inside the restored LaBelle Theatre, across from the South Charleston Library. This museum is dedicated to preserving artifacts related to the area's culture and history; they also show many films about the region.

To get there, take exit 56 off I-64 to MacCorkle Avenue SW, then turn left onto 4th Ave. and left onto D Street.

Exhibitions are open Monday through Friday from 9 a.m. to 4:30 p.m. Archives available by appointment.

Battle of Hurricane Bridge!

M. V. B. Edens, Co. A. 13th Va. Vol.[2]

Between a high hill and circuitous ridge,
Is the neat little town, known as Hurricane Bridge,
Or at least, 'twas a neat little village before -
The rebellion arose in the bright days of yore.

But rebellion has banished those pleasures, so sweet,
And the wail of despair is now heard in the street -
The many fine buildings in ashes are laid
The wealth of the inmates forever decayed.

The 13th Virginia is camped near this town,
Who in a late battle have won great renown.
The regiment is formed of a brave set of boys,
Who accomplish their work without making much noise.

But Albert G. Jenkins not aware of that fact,
Came early one morning to make an attack,
With a yard of white cotton unfurled to the breeze,
His staff came into camp, while Jenkins stayed behind trees.

'Twas Samuels who brought in the banner of truce.
Says Johnson, to surrender I this morning refuse.
In the time which is given to my works I'll repair.
And give you a battle on principles fair.

When cool as an iceberg we fell into line.
To defend the bright stars which on our banner doth shine,

[2]*Point Pleasant Weekly Register*, April 30, 1863

And to hold our position ast Hurricane Bridge,
In spite of the rebs on each neighboring ridge.

For Jenkins marched forth with his menacing host
To capture or drive us away from our post,
He threw his men round on the top of each hill
To make us surrender or fly at his will.

He thought with his men on the left and the right,
He would capture our squad without having to fight,
And with Yankee clothing he his men would equip,
And thus would secure successful his trip.

But Albert was much disappointed to find
To surrender that morning we were not inclined
Then he told all his men to prepare for the blow
And soon they'd conquer the insolent foe.

From each hill top they fired on the 13th in vain,
For each at his post did boldly remain.
For the space of four hours he fought very hard
But his incessant firing we not much did regard.

Like Jeff. Davis' scrip that's more plenty than good,
They sent in their lead from each neighboring wood
Like the insects that sing in the long days of June,
The balls from the rebs almost whistled a [tune?]

But is was not sufficient to induce us to dance,
It was like Mason in England or Slidell in France,
Who after they made known their treacherous plan,
Have to end their hard labor just where they began.

With stomach's quite empty and feet without shoes,
Each felt like a bankrupt with a spell of the blues,

Like a dishonored guest ere the bankquet [sic] is o'er
Arrives at the feast and is kept from the door.

They knew in our camp were crackers, coffee and meat,
And they longed to get in to get something to eat.
Like Cruse's man Friday, who on the mountain did stand,
And beheld in the distance, his own native land.

With obtsacles [sic] in front which he could not surmount
Was not able to settle the lengthy account,
And fell ere he crossed o'er the dark rolling wave
And found in the deep sea a watery grave.

So Jenkins after giving us a hard shower of hail
And finding with muskets he could not prevail
Sent out his command to retreat from the field,
For the 13th Virginia was too stubborn to yield.

Being tired and hungry, they left in disgust,
Aware of the fact that Albert won't do to trust;
He promised to give them both food and attire,
In short everything that a reb could desire.

Except a good thrashing they left as they came
With nothing to brighten Jeff. Davis' fame;
And Jenkins found out that one blunder he made
In seeking for sunshine he found nought but shade.

Chapter 3

Mound Indians

The Adena Indians arrived in the Kanawha County area around 1000 B.C., and resided here until around 1650. Their heritage was a mystery to many who believed that Native Americans could not have been so advanced or skilled; some said they came from Mexico, some said they came from Europe, and some referred to them as the Lost Tribes of Israel.

The mound that is located in South Charleston is the second largest in the state, out of 50 or so known Adena mounds in the area. It is also one of the best-known mounds and is called the Criel Mound, in honor of a family who owned a farm there once upon a time.

The Criel Mound is 175 Feet in diameter at the base, and 35 feet high. The Smithsonian Institution examined it in 1883-1884 and found the mound to be made of numerous layers. Near the top was a wagon load of large, flat stones. Beneath the stones was a four foot deep vault, containing a skeleton and a spearhead. Six feet further down was another skeleton; three more feet down, another. After another few feet there was a walnut vault 12x12x8. This vault contained five skeletons of people who had been buried alive. One of them was 7'6" tall—a giant even by today's standards. These skeletons were accompanied by spearheads, bracelets, tools, and beads.

The Smithsonian Institution spent over $5,000 on the study of the mound; at the completion of it, Cyrus Thomas published his book Report on the Mound Explorations of the Bureau of Ethnology which proved that the Mound Builders were not European or Israelites, but were American Indians.

The mound was used as late as 1650, but may have been started around 250-150 B.C. it's one of only 50 conical shaped mounds in the Charleston area; the industrialization of the area over the past 140 years has destroyed nearly all of them. You can visit the mound at 2402 Woodland Avenue, Charleston, West Virginia.

Mound builders thrived along the Mississippi and Ohio River Valleys. These mounds were constructed by laborers carrying earth in baskets by hand. The building was overseen by nobles, priests, and dignitaries. Often they were added to many years after previous building had ceased.

The Adena were located in current day Kentucky, Ohio, West Virginia, Indiana, Pennsylvania, and southwestern NY. They cultivated crops like gourds, pumpkins, sunflowers, and goosefoot and tobacco. They were hunters and gatherers but they were not nomads. The Adena built mounds from 20 to 300 feet in diameter. Many of the people were cremated, then buried in small log tombs. They were big traders, as seen by the fact that many of the materials found in the mounds weren't from the area; the mica was from the Carolinas, the shells from the Gulf of Mexico, and the copper from the western Great Lakes region.

If you go there...

The Criel Mound is centered in Staunton Park. This park is fairly small, but beautiful; it is used as a gathering center for many arts and crafts shows, revivals, religious services, and carnivals. Phone 304-746-5552.

An Indian Pow-wow is held year round at the South Charleston Indian Mound, featuring authentic music, food, dancing and storytelling to celebrate the Native American Indian Heritage. For more information please call 800-238-9488.

The second Saturday in September, the mound is the site of the Festival of Arts and Crafts, with over 230 vendors, music, food, and entertainment.

It is believed that these Woodland Indians had no villages, but eventually they banded together and became the Fort Ancient Indians. They built large villages along the River, constructed in circles with stockades of large poles surrounding them. Houses were placed inside the stockade in one or two rows. Archaeologists have noted that their diet changed somewhat, switching from nuts and seeds to the freshwater clams and mussels from the river. Eventually these Indians were driven out by other tribes like the Iroquois, who used the entire area as a hunting ground.

Traders in the Area

In the 1700s, French fur traders often camped along the river. The traders were eager to establish strong ties with the Indians; after all, who could best supply them with the furs they needed for their business? This relationship was often created by marrying an Indian woman—quickly giving the trader trading rights with the tribe. Embracing the lifestyle gave them the ability to learn the language, or at least have an interpreter as well.

More Indian History

In Fayette County (formed from part of present day Kanawha County) an old stone wall nearly ten miles long was discovered in 1872 by employees of the C&O railroad, who were laying railway in the area. The wall was about six feet tall and enclosed over 300 acres. The stones that made the wall were huge, some weighing hundreds of pounds. They found many human skeletons and animal remains. Indian legend said that the wall was built by an ancient race of white men, presumably before the Native Americans arrived. There have been many other theories about why the wall contained such huge number of skeletons; it could have been built for fortification, religious purposes, or even for taming or training horses or other animals.

Indians never really chose to leave the area; instead, they were driven back from the river, as were the numerous buffalo, deer, elk, bears, panthers and wolves that inhabited the fertile land. It is thought that hydrophobia killed most of the wildlife. In the days of the Indians, there were no crows, blackbirds, or song birds; those were brought with the white people.

Rocking Communication

Devils Tea Table rock located in Kanawha City is a natural rock formation that visitors won't want to miss. It is said that it was a smoke signal point for the Indian community for over 300 years. The formation is eleven feet from the base to the projection of the top, and 15 X 24 feet on top.

The Devil's Tea Table is one of the sights you can see during a visit to Little Creek Park, off Spring Hill Avenue on the West side of South Charleston.

If you go there...

Enjoy the natural beauty and changing scenery throughout the year. The park features hiking trails, "Devil's Tea Table", an old saw mill and a natural spring. There are eleven picnic shelters available for rent, restrooms, and recreational equipment. The shelters have electricity, grills and fireplaces. Open March 1 through October 31 daily from 8:30 a.m. to 10:30 p.m.

An Indian Mystery

At an area called Three Points, just below the mouth of Camp Creek, two things happened with regularity. The first was that the spring floods always overflowed the creek into the Kanawha River. The second was that a group of Indians made a pilgrimage every fifth year.

Was it a religious meeting? Were they paying tribute to someone—and if so, whom? No one knows, but in the early 1950s the Indians suddenly stopped showing up. Perhaps the tribe had died out, or perhaps the debt had been paid.

The Murder of Cornstalk

The year was 1777. The Indians were worried by the rapid settlement by the settlers, which the Indians saw as a sign of aggression.

One of the most significant battles between the Shawnee and the pioneers took place in 1773, when a land speculator named Michael Cresap led a group of volunteers from Fort Fincastle at Wheeling and raided several Shawnee towns, even murdering a peaceful Indian chief who had been baptized and lived peacefully among the settlers. The Indian retaliated by killing about 132 western Virginians.

The Earl of Dunmore, who was also the Governor of Virginia John Murray made a plan to crush the Shawnee. Cornstalk led 1200 men against Dunmore's troops at Point Pleasant on October 10, 1774. The Shawnee retreated, and as a condition of the resulting Treaty of Camp Charlotte the Delaware, Shawnee and Mingo tribes gave up all claims to the land lying south of the Ohio River . The battle of Point Pleasant effectively eliminated Native Americans as a contending force from the frontier for the first three years of the Revolutionary War. They began to become hostile to the frontier settlements. The pioneers were nervous and troubled.

In August 1775 the Shawnee, Ottawa, Mingo, Delaware, Seneca, Wyandot, and Pottawatomie had agreed to the Treaty of Pittsburgh, which created an Indian boundary in the Ohio River and also stated that the Indians agreed to neutrality. Soon though the treaty was no longer valid; Henry Hamilton, a British Negotiator, met with tribal leaders at Detroit and convinced most Native Americans to join in the efforts on the British side. Initially, they enjoyed success against the Colonists.

Cornstalk, whose name was Hokolekwa in the Shawnee language, was a prominent leader around the time of the American Revolution. Cornstalk was a reluctant war leader; he knew that his people could not stop the Virginian invasion of Ohio on their own. His tribe wanted to make a stand, however, so he led the way.

Cornstalk was apparently a great orator—in fact, it is said that a Virginia officer referred to him as a better one than Patrick Henry and Richard Henry Lee.

Cornstalk wanted his people to remain neutral in the American Revolutionary war. Many of the Shawnee however were of the belief that the British would help them to reclaim the land they had lost to the pioneers. All the Shawnee tribes, other than Cornstalk's, wanted to join the British. Cornstalk knew that, regardless of what his opinion was, if the Indian nation went in a certain direction he and his tribe would follow.

In 1777 Cornstalk visited Fort Randolph (located at present day Point Pleasant). He was there on a peaceful mission, as he made no secret of the fact that he wanted to maintain neutrality. However, the fort commander, Captain Arbuckle, had decided to take the Shawnee hostage, so he detained Cornstalk. Arbuckle thought that by doing so, he could prevent the Indian Nation from joining sides with the British.

Cornstalk's son, Elinipsico, began to wonder about his father's well-being, so he journeyed to the fort to check on him. At the very moment he called out to his father from across the river, Cornstalk was delineating a map of the country with a piece of chalk on the floor. He gladly embraced his son and invited him to stay with him.

In the meantime, Colonel Skillern had gathered a small party of about 40 men to travel to Point Pleasant from Augusta and Botetourt. This party made its way down the Kanawha planning to "chastise" the Shawnee in order to reinforce their neutrality.

During the trip two young men named Hamilton and Gilmore were deer hunting when Gilmore was ambushed and scalped by a party of Indians. Gilmore's relative, Captain Arbuckle, and other members of their corps were standing on the opposite riverbank when this happened, so they rushed to Hamilton's aid via canoe, bringing Gilmore's maimed body back with them—much to the relief of Hamilton, who probably thought his own death was imminent.

The group of soldiers, angry now over the senseless death, shouted "let us kill the Indians" and rushed back to the fort, where they each took their gun in hand. They executed Cornstalk, his son Elinipsico, and injured another Shawnee called Redhawk.

It is said that the interpreter's wife, who had been a prisoner to the Indians herself, heard the men threatening to kill the Indians, so she ran to warn Cornstalk and Elinipsico. In fact, she said, the Indians had been seen with Elinipsico the day before. He completely denied the charge and was terrified. His father told him that the Great Man Above had sent him there to be with Cornstalk on the day of his death.

When the men rushed in the doorway, Cornstalk rose and nearly instantly took eight bullets. His son was shot where he still sat, on a stool. The other Indian with them died a slow, miserable death from his wounds.

Patrick Henry and other political leaders were concerned about the murder; they had faith in Cornstalk as their only hope of keeping the Shawnee at a neutral stance. Henry, in fact, called Cornstalk's killers "vile assassins" and took them to trial. All were acquitted, even though most of the pioneers thought the murders were a total disgrace.

On the day he was killed Cornstalk met with a council, stating that he fully expected to join the British like all the other Indians. He seemed dejected, and repeatedly said, "You may kill me if you please; I can die but once, and it is all one to me... now or another time." One hour later he was murdered.

Point Pleasant did not thrive for many years. Superstition held that the town was cursed with the murder of perhaps the greatest Indian chief that ever lived. There was no church; no businesses could thrive; there were reports of ghosts. Eventually, however, the stigma faded as the old generations were replaced by newer ones.

Cornstalk was buried near Fort Randolph, where he was killed. But in 1840, his remains were moved to the Mason County courthouse grounds. When the courthouse was being razed and rebuilt, the decision was made to move the grave to Tu-Endie-Wei Park at the intersection of the Ohio and Kanawha Rivers. The name means "Point between two waters." Ironically, the park holds a monument honoring the very soldiers Cornstalk warred against.

If you go there...

The four acre state park contains an 84-foot granite monument that honors the Virginia militiamen, as well as a memorial tablet to honor Cornstalk and another honoring "Mad" Anne Bailey (see page 192 for her story).

Also located inside the park is the oldest hewn log home in the Kanawha Valley. It features period displays of authentic furnishings.

Tu-Endie-Wei State Park is open year-round. The museum is open from May through October.

Hours:
Mon-Sat 10:00 a.m. - 4:30 p.m.

Sun 1:00 p.m. - 4:30 p.m.
Open holidays. (304) 675-0869

Krodel Park contains Fort Randolph, a replica of the eighteenth century installation that once stood at Point Pleasant. The fort is owned by the cit of Point Pleasant and maintained by a committee of volunteers. For more information visit http://www.pointpleasantwv.org.

Kanawha Falls Discovered 1671

It is said that the first white men to ever set foot in Western Virginia were Captain Thomas Batts, Thomas Wood, and Robert Fallam. These men were sent on an exploration by Royal Governor William Berkeley of the Virginia Colony and they discovered the Kanawha Falls in September, 1671. They marked their initials on the trees above, then battled their way through the native weeds and thistles in order to get down to the river. They likened it to the James River and believed it to be about 3 feet deep.

Kanawha Falls, now a popular fishing spot, is located about 35 miles southeast of Charleston, near the Gauley Bridge. The river is wide and the falls are scenic, set against a backdrop of the West Virginia Mountains. A small park there offers fishing, a boat ramp, and a parking area.

Also at Kanawha Falls you can see Van Bibbers Rock. It is said that the Native Americans called the rock War-kun-gee-tah, meaning "the far away look out." The boulder juts out 100 feet over a very active whirlpool at the foot of the Kanawha Falls. Reuben Van Bibbers jumped off of it during the early part of the American

Revolution to escape a band of Indians who were chasing him. His wife saw his leap and managed to reach him via canoe, rescuing him from the rough, swirling water. Van Bibber was an oddity in the area; he was said to be the first white settler to build a cabin in the area. He was also supposed to have kept a pet bear that he raised from a cub.

If you go there…

You can reach the Falls via US-60 and WV-16. Two miles west of Gauley Bridge is a bridge crossing the Kanawha River. Cross it and then turn left and follow Kanawha Road to the Kanawha Falls Park.

There are three ways to reach Gauley Bridge:

From Charleston - east on US-60; follow US-60 up the Kanawha River to Gauley Bridge.

From I-79 - exit 57 to US-19 south to US-60 (17 miles south of Summerville). Turn right and follow 60 West to Gauley Bridge.

From Beckley - US-19 north across the New River Bridge. About 26 miles, turn left on US-60 and go to Gauley Bridge.

English Women in Kanawha County

It is believed that Mary Ingles and Betty Draper were the very first English women to pass through present-day Kanawha County. Mary Ingles, a vibrant, attractive young lady was married to William Ingles. They lived in Draper's Meadows, a beautiful idyllic location that is now a part of the Virginia Tech campus. They had two children, ages 4 and 2, and Mary was expecting another baby any day. The family lived peaceably on

Indian hunting ground; bands of Shawnee hunters often stopped in for food or shelter.

But in 1755, the French and Indian war was imminent. The Shawnee were aligned with the French against the English colonists. Unbeknownst to the isolated Virginia settlers, several battles had already been fought further north.

On July 8, 1755, Captain Wildcat, a Shawnee leader, and about 30 Indians attacked and killed many of the settlers. They took Mary, her children, and her sister-in-law Bettie captive. William was spared, as he was not at home at the time.

Mary was taken westward toward the Ohio River by her captors, and on the third day she gave birth to a daughter. The trip was exhausting and dangerous; the Indians continued to kill and scalp settlers along the way, sometimes putting their severed heads into sacks to bring along on the journey.

When the Indians reached the Kanawha River, they crossed to the east side and began manufacturing salt at the spring to take with them to their Ohio village. They remained there for several weeks, resting and feasting on the abundant game that visited the salt licks, giving Mary an opportunity to grow stronger. Mary helped the Indians to make the salt by boiling brine. It was her opinion that her doctoring, cooking, sewing, and other cooperation would help to secure her tenuous position, as well as that of her children, with the Indians. This probably made her not only one of the first white people to enter the Kanawha Valley, but also one of the first to make salt.

After about 20 days of marching, the party reached Point Pleasant, where they turned downstream and eventually went to the main Shawnee town of Chillicothe. There Mary's children were taken from her and sent to live at another Shawnee village. Mary became depressed, barely able to do the cooking and hard work the Indians expected of her.

In October, Mary and an elderly Dutch woman managed to escape from the Indians. They stole a horse and made their way across the Big Sandy River (near present Louisa, Kentucky).Their moccasins wore out along the way; their clothes became tattered. Finally they reached the Kanawha River just as the temperature fell and snow began to fall. The Dutch woman became delusional, probably due to hunger and exposure of the long journey; she threatened to kill Mary.

Mary knew her only chance was to hide from the old woman, so she found an Indian canoe and crossed to the opposite shore. There she slept in a cabin and found some turnips and kale to eat. She set out again across high mountains, braving snow and bitter West Virginia cold. Finally, six weeks after her escape, she came to the cabin of her good friends, the Harmans. Mary called out to Adam Harman and then collapsed on the ground. By some reports, she weighed barely 70 pounds. She had traveled 450 miles over rough terrain to return to the Blacksburg area. At only 23 years old, her lovely auburn hair had turned to solid white during the journey, which remained that way till her death at age 83.

Mary Ingles' escape and her subsequent return through the wilderness to Virginia was an inspiration to all pioneers on the frontier. Her saga was memorialized in Alexander Thom's best-selling novel, "Follow the River." Earl Hobson Smith wrote an outdoor drama based on her life, "The Long Way Home," which is still produced each summer in Radford; ABC used it as the basis of a made-for-television movie which aired in 1995.

The Mary Draper Ingles Trail

This trail, a part of the Kanawha State Forest, is an opportunity to visit terrain, flora, and fauna like that which Mary Ingles probably encountered during her long journey home. The trail is marked by yellow blazes and can be reached via McGhee Road off of Trace Fork Road, or by Middlelick Road. For more information contact the Forest Office at 304-558-3500.

The Founding of a City

The land where Charleston is now located was granted to Colonel Thomas Bullitt in 1773 in return for his services during the French and Indian War. He sold the land to his brother Cuthbert, of Maryland, who subsequently transferred it to his son Cuthbert of Prince William County, Virginia.

Charles Clendenin was a settler in the Greenbrier Valley around 1780. He had four sons who were all accomplished soldiers. His son Colonel George Clendenin of the Virginia Rangers purchased land at the mouth of the Elk River in about 1787. One year later he settled there along with his family, including his father.

In 1788 these men began to build the city: first a block-house, which was a dwelling as well as the fort, courthouse, and jail. There were 7 houses by 1790. This was later to become Fort Lee, named for then-General Henry "light Horse Harry" Lee, who later became the Governor of Virginia. Fort Lee was located at what is now the corner of Brooks Street and Kanwha Boulevard in Charleston. It served as a frontier outpost, protecting white settlers from raiding Indians.

The fort soon grew in population and was called either "The town at the Mouth of the Elk" or "Clendenin Settlement." It had 12 houses. in December 1794, the General Assembly declared that the forty acres of land, "the property of George Clendenin, at the mouth of Elk river in the County of Kanawha, as the same are already laid off into lots and streets, shall be established a town by the name of Charles Town." It is said that the name was in honor of the father of the Clendenin brothers, Charles. The pound, shilling, and pence were the currency denominations used in the town even up until 1899.

Point Pleasant and the Revolutionary War

The Battle of Point Pleasant took place on October 10, 1774. it was the very first battle that was brought on by American Colonists in order to defend the colonies.

The battle was not so newsworthy at the time, because General Lewis and his troops were on their way to Camp Union, so they had not made a roster. It was facts that came out afterward that showed the country the importance of the battle as it occurred.

Lewis believed that Lord Dunmore was taking part in enemy actions; so he refused to obey Dunmore's orders, thus becoming the first American officer to Disobey a (superior) British officer.

Governor Dunmore and General Lewis were organizing their armies, planning to unite and march to the Indian towns to either conquer them or create a peace agreement. Dunmore took most of the army on a long detour past Fort Pitt; at Fort Pitt he met with some of the Indian Chiefs.

Dunmore must have never intended to meet Lewis at the Kanawha rvier, as agreed; instead, he marched into several indian towns.

Lewis was given messsages that ordered him, not once but twice in the same day, to stop marching (he was was crossing the river to join Lord Dunmore). Dunmore clearly did not want the help of General Lewis with his negotiations.

During the battle of 1122 men, about 44 were killed. Many considered this battle the true beginning of the Revolutionary War.

Later, In 1883, one writer wrote that it was a "well known fact" that the British were trying to incite hostility in the Indians. Lord Dunmore would have enjoyed getting the Indians to join with them, because it meant they would not be subject to the colonists'whims.

Daniel Boone was here

Daniel Boone, famous frontiersman and founder of Kentucky, resided with his family in Kanawha County for seven years, from 1788-1795. They lived in a two-room log cabin in the Kanawha City section of Charleston. Daniel was a surveyor while living in the area, later leaving the area to move to Missouri. He was commissioned a Lieutenant Colonel in the Kanawha County militia and served under the command of Colonel George Clendenin. In fact, Boone and Colonel Clendenin represented Kanawha County in the General Assembly in 1791. It is said that Boone walked all the way to Richmond.

> Daniel Boone Park, 4 acres, is located on Kanawha Boulevard East (Route 60) which offers picnic facilities, boating, fishing, and a beautiful view of the Kanawha River.

The Fort Under Attack – Mad Anne Bailey

Anne Bailey was the wife of a British Soldier who came to America in the 1770s to help "tame" the rebels. Lots were drawn to see whose wives would accompany them, and Bailey's wife was able to come with him. When her husband was killed near the close of the campaign, around 1780, and she vowed she would avenge his death. She wanted to make the wilderness safe for others, especially her young son, William.

Anne took to living in the West Virginia woods, hunting, riding, and fighting like a man. It was said that she was overjoyed with the adventure of living like a wild rebel soldier. Her language was coarse and often profane, and her flask of liquor was never far from reach. She wore a thick handkerchief around her head, leaving her matted hair wild and savage beneath it. She carried a tomahawk, a scalping knife, and a rifle. She wore buckskin leggings under her petticoat, apparently the singular feminine detail of her appearance.

The Indians were the ones who dubbed her "Mad Anne", apparently believing she was possessed of an evil spirit since she could ride through Indian territory without harm. Perhaps it was her high level of intelligence that kept her from harm; once, when Indians were chasing her, Anne simply jumped off her horse and hid from them in a hollow log. The Indians stole the horse. Later that night, Anne sneaked into their camp and stole it back.

In 1791, a runner appeared at Fort Lee to warn them that an attack was imminent. The fort found itself very low on ammunition. It is said that Anne Bailey jumped on her black horse, Liverpool, and rode 100 miles alone through the wilderness to Fort Savannah, located at Lewisburg to get gunpowder for Charleston. This was a singularly dangerous route that didn't even have roads to guide her.

Anne became a hero that night, and was a favorite with settlers in every cabin she visited; after all, it was a new country with a new form of society. The exciting stories shared by "Mother Anne" often brought tears to the eyes of her rapt audience. Anne's heroic ride was commemorated in the poem, "Anne Bailey's Ride", by Charles Robb. She died at Gallipolis in 1825; in 1901, her bones were moved to the park at Point Pleasant, where a marker commemorates her life. The following poem was written as a memorial to her.

Anne Bailey's Ride

By Charles Robb

The Army at Gauley Bridge,
At Mountain Cove and Sewell Ridge:
Our tents were pitched on hill and dell
From Charleston Height to Cross Lane fell;
Our camp-fires blazed on every route,
From Red House point to Camp Lookout;
On every rock our sentries stood,
Our scouts held post in every wood,
And every path was stained with blood
From Scary creek to Gauley flood.
'Twas on a bleak autumnal day,
When not a single sunbeam's ray
Could struggle through the dripping skies
To cheer our melancholy eyes-
Whilst heavy clouds, like funeral palls,
Hung o'er Kanawha's foaming falls
And shrouded all the mountain green
With dark, foreboding, misty screen.
All through the weary livelong day

Our troops had marched the
mountain way;
and in the gloomy eventide
Had pitched their tents by the river's side;
And as the darkness settled o'er
The hill and vale and river shore,
We gathered round the camp-fire bright,
That threw its glare on the misty night;
And each some tale or legend told
To while away the rain and cold.
Thus, one a tale of horror told
That made the very blood run cold;
One spolce of suff'ring and of wrong;
Another sang a mountain song;
One spoke of home, and happy years,
Till down his swarthy cheeks the tears
Slow dripping, glistened in the light
That glared upon the misty night;
While others sat in silence deep,
Too sad for mirth, yet scorned to weep.
Then spake a hardy mountaineer
(His beard was long, his eye was clear:
And Clear his voice, of metal tone,
Just such as all would wish to own)-
"I've heard a legend old," he said,
"Of one who used these paths to tread
Long years ago, when fearful strife
Sad havoc made of human life;
A deed of daring bravely done,
A feat of honor nobly won;
And what in story's most uncommon,
An army saved by a gentle woman.

"'Twas in that dark and bloody time (1791)
When savage craft and tory crime
From Northern lake to Southern flood,
Had drenched the western world
with blood.
And in this wild, romantic glen
Encamped a host of savage men,
Whose mad'ning war-whoop,
loud and high,
Was answered by the panthers cry.
"The pale-faced settlers all had fled,
Or murdered were in lonely bed;
Whilst hut and cabin, blazing high,
With crimson decked the midnight sky.
"I said the settlers all had fled-
Their pathway down the valley led
To where the Elk's bright crystal waves
On dark Kanawha's bosom laves,
There safety sought, and respite brief,
And in Fort Charleston found relief;
Awhile they bravely met their woes,
And kept at bay their savage foes.
'Thus days and weeks the warfare waged,
In fury still the conflict raged;
Still fierce and bitter grew the strife
Where every foeman fought for life.
Thus day by day the siege went on,
Till three long, weary weeks were gone;
And then the mournful word was passed
That every day might be their last;
The word was whispered soft and slow,
The magazine was getting low.

They loaded their rifles one by one,
And
then-the powder all was gone!
They
stood like men in calm despair,
No friendly aid could reach them there;
Their doom was sealed, the scalping knife
And burning stake must end the strife.
One forlorn hope alone remained,
That distant aid might yet be gained
If trusty messenger should go
Through forest wild, and savage foe,
And safely there should bear report,
And succor bring from distant Fort.
But who should go-the venture dare?
The woodsmen quailed in mute despair,
In vain the call to volunteer;
The bravest blenched with silent fear.
Each gloomy brow and labored breath,
Proclaimed the venture worse than death.
Not long the fatal fact was kept;
But through the Fort the secret crept
Until it reached the ladies' hall,
There like a thunderbolt to fall.
Each in terror stood amazed,
And silent on the other gazed;
No word escaped-there fell no tear-
But all was hushed in mortal fear;
All hope of life at once had fled,
And filled each soul with nameless dread.
But one (Anne
Bailey) who stood amid

the rest,
The bravest, fairest, and the best
Of all that graced the cabin hall,
First broke the spell of terror's thrall.
Her step was firm, her features fine,
Of Mortal mould the most divine;
But why describe her graces fair,
Her form her mien, her stately air?
Nay hold! my pen, I will not dare!
'Twas Heaven's image mirrored there.
She spoke no word, of fear or boast,
But smiling, passed the sentry post;
And half in hope, and half in fear,
She whispered in her husband's ear,
The sacrifice her soul would make
Her friends to save from brand and stake.
A noble charger standing nigh,
Of spirit fine, and metal high,
Was saddled well, and girted strong,
With cord, and loop, and leathem thong,
For her was led in haste from stall,
Upon whose life depended all.
Her friends she gave a parting brief,
No time was there for idle grief;
Her husband's hand a moment wrung,
then lightly to the saddle sprung;
And followed by the prayers and tears,
The kindling hopes, and boding fears
Of those who seemed the sport of fate,
She dashed beyond the op'ning gate;
Like a birdling free, on pinion light,
Commenced her long and weary flight.

"The foeman saw the op'ning gate,
And thought with victory elate
To rush within the portal rude,
And in his dark and savage mood
To end the sanguinary strife
With tomahawk and scalping-knife.
But lo! a lady! fair and bright,
And seated on a charger light,
Bold-and free—as one immortal-
Bounded o'er the op'ning portal.
Each savage paused in mute surprise,
And gazed with wonder-staring eyes;
'A squaw! a squaw! the chieftain cries,
('A squaw! a squaw!' the host replies;)
With lightening speed
and catch the fawn.'
Her pathway up the valley led,
Like frightened deer the charger fled,
And urged along by whip and rein,
The quick pursuit was all in vain,
A hundred bended bows were sprung,
A thousand savage echoes rung
But far too short the arrows fell
All harmless in the mountain dell;
'To horse! to horse!' the chieftain cried,
They mount in haste and madly ride.
Along the rough, uneven way,
The pathway of the lady lay;
Whilst long and loud the savage yell
Re-echoed through the mountain fell.
She heeded not the danger rife,
But rode as one who rides for life;

Still onward in her course she bore
Along the dark Kanawha's shore,
Through tangled wood and rocky way,
Nor paused to rest at close of day.
Like skimming cloud before the wind
Soon left the rabble far behind.
From bended tree above the road
The flying charger wildly trode,
Amid the evening's gath'ring gloom,
The panther's shriek, the voice of doom
In terror fell upon the ear,
And quickened every pulse with fear.
But e'en the subtle panther's bound,
To reach his aim
too slow was found;
And headlong falling on the rock,
Lay crushed and mangled in the shock.
The prowling wolf then scents his prey,
And rushing on with angry bay,
With savage growl and quickening bound
He clears the rough and rugged ground;
And closing fast the lessening space
That all too soon must end the race,
With sharpened teeth that glittered white
As stars amid the gloomy night-
With foaming jaws had almost grasped
The lovely had that firmly clasped,
And well had used the whip and rein,
But further effort now were vain;
Another bound-a movement more-
And then the struggle all were o'er.
'Twas in a steep and rocky gorge

Along the river's winding verge,
Just where the foaming torrent falls
Far down through adamantine halls.
And then comes circling round and round,
As loath to leave the enchanted ground.
Just there a band of wand'rmg braves
Had pitched their tents beside the waves.
The sun long since had sunk to rest,
And long the light had faded west-
When all were startled by the sound
Of howling wolf and courser's bound,
That onward came, with fearful clang,
Whose echoes round the mountain rang;
The frightened wolf in wild surprise
A moment paused-with glaring eyes
In terror gazed upon the flame,
Then backward fled the way he came.
Each wondering savage saw with fear
The charger come like frightened deer;
With weary gait, and heavy tramp,
The foaming steed dashed through
the camp
And onward up the valley bear
His queenly rider, brave and fair.
Stilt on, and on, through pathless wood-
They swim the Gauley's swollen flood,
And climb Mount Tompkins' lofty brow,
More wild and rugged far than now,
Still onward held their weary flight
Beyond the Hawk's Nest's Giddy Height;
And often chased through lonely glen
By savage beast or savage men-

Thus like some weary, hunted dove
The woman sped through
'Mountain Cove,'
The torrent crossed without a bridge,
And scaled the heights of Sewell Ridge,
And still the wild, beleaguered road
With heavy tramp the charger trode,
Nor paused amid his weary flight
Throughout the long and dreary night.
And bravely rode the woman there
Where few would venture,
Few would dare
Amid the cheering light of day
To tread the wild beleaguered way;
And as the morning sunbeams fall
O'er hill and dale, and sylvan hall,
Far in the distance, dim and blue,
The friendly Fort (Lewisburg) arose to view,
Whose portal soon the maiden gains
With slackened speed and loosened reins
And voice whose trembling accents tell,
Of journey ridden long and well.
"The succor thus so nobly sought,
To Charleston Fort was timely brought;
Whilst Justice, on the scroll of fame,
In letters bold, engraved her name."

Chapter 4

A City is Born

The story of the Capitol

The story of West Virginia's Capital actually begins in Wheeling, not Charleston. The first State Legislature met in Wheeling beginning in 1863. The capital of West Virginia intermittently moved from Wheeling to Charleston. In order to move, the state officials met at the levee in Wheeling. They boarded a steamer named *The Mountain Boy,* which was already packed with state records and other files, and moved down the Ohio River to the Kanawha River to Charleston. The legislature probably approved the move because Charleston agreed to provide $50,000 toward the cost of constructing a new capital building.

The first Charleston Capitol building was built courtesy of Dr. John P. Hale, local physician, at Capitol and Lee Streets. During construction, state officials used churches, schools and other buildings as temporary offices. The three story building was completed in 1870 and was the state Capitol until May of 1875, when once again steamers carried officials back to Wheeling. In fact, Charleston citizens filed a temporary court injunction to halt the removal of state records, but were unsuccessful. The Supreme Court did not back them.

In Wheeling the government first returned to the original building, the Linsly Institute, then moved into a stone building donated by the city. Some people were so unhappy about the move that they paid orators to speak against the move; one of the orators who lobbied to move the capitol back to Charleston was Booker T. Washington.

Eventually the unrest that resulted from the choice of Wheeling as a capital city grew, so West Virginians were given a statewide referendum with three choices to vote on: Charleston, Clarksburg, and Martinsburg. Wheeling was not one of the options. Voters chose Charleston.

In 1877 the state's citizens voted on Charleston as their capitol's location and in 1885 the second capitol building was opened. This time the move was made by using two steamers, the Bell Prince and the Chesapeake, and a barge in tow named Nick Crawley.

The new building was located on the same grounds as the first Charleston Capitol. It occupied an entire city block, from Washington and Lee to Capitol and Dickinson Streets. The Capitol Annex at Hale and Lee was added a few years later.

This structure, a picturesque building with a clock tower that was covered in vines, was completely destroyed by fire in 1921. Fortunately the state records were housed in the Capitol Annex, so they were saved.

The building contained thousands of rounds of ammunition that had been confiscated exploded, fueling the savage fire.

Another temporary structure was quickly built in only 42 days. It cost $225,000 and was created of wood and wallboard at the Daniel Boone Hotel site. It was recognized for the "Pasteboard capitol" that it was, as plans were already under way to make a change.

Nine days after the fire, Governor Cornwell's term of office was drawing to a close. He spoke to the Legislature about the need for a new building, properly designed to contain the two houses of the legislature, committee rooms, offices, and a second building in close proximity that would contain the boards and departments. The governor was granted power to appoint a Capitol building commission. a commission was formed to create a building "the likes of which no one has ever seen." The temporary structure burned down in 1927.

Several sites were considered, one of which was the Charleston Memorial Hospital's current location. Eventually, near the end of 1921, the current site was chosen and the architect, Cass Gilbert, went to work designing the complex.

In addition to the West Virginia State Capitol, Gilbert designed the "skyscraper", a sixty-story Woolworth building in New York City in 1912. He designed numerous other state capitols, the US. Treasury Annex, the U.S. Chamber of commerce building, and other insurance buildings, bank buildings, and a host of other buildings.

Construction Begins

Building the Capitol at this location involved the purchase of 65 pieces of property from California Avenue to Duffy Street. The homes that were located here were moved; some went to Washington Street, and some to Quarrier and its cross streets. Some of the other homes were razed, and a few remained as temporary offices during construction. A number of homes were literally taken from their foundations, secured onto barges, and moved across the river to South Ruffner. The homes that were moved this way were not even packed up, in today's sense; furniture and its contents were left as they stood, the door locked, and incredibly, most survived the move. A 1923 newspaper article reported that there was no damage to the brick, and even the gas mantles remained intact. These moves cost up to $5,000 and took from three days to three weeks to complete. Of 50 homes that were moved, only two or three were said to be dismantled first.

One important part of the plans for the complex was the location of the Governor's Mansion. This was designed by Charleston architect Walter F. Martens, who consulted closely with Cass Gilbert and completed the structure in 1925. Governor Morgan lived there for one week before the end of his term of office in March, 1925.

The Capitol building commission authorized construction of the present structure. It was completed in 1932 and encompassed 16 acres.

When excavation began, the earth that was removed in order to create a west wing basement was placed into the open holes left by the removal of structures on the site. Trees, bushes, and shrubs were boxed and saved for future use on the grounds. The Capitol Building is made of limestone laid over a steel frame. The materials were brought in via railway, requiring 700 carloads to transport the limestone and 160 cars of steel.

The pillars at the north and south entrances of the building each weigh 86 tons. They support Roman Corinthian-style porticos. At the east and west entrances are sculpted Greek and Roman figures: Prometheus, Zeus, Fortuna, and nine others.

The capitol dome is gilded in 23 karat gold leaf. It was gilded in 1923, then re-gilded over a three-year period from 1988 to 1991 at a cost of $500,000. The dome is topped by a bronze staff with a golden eagle poised upon its edge.

The Capitol building is as impressive now as when it was constructed. It is made from Indiana limestone in an Italian Renaissance style. It was said to have required three stages of construction at a cost of about $10 million. Governor William Conley dedicated the present capitol building in 1932.

On the Inside

The West wing was completed first, and most officials moved in; however the Treasurer, W.S. Johnson, refused his office. He felt that the safe that had been built would not be adequately secure to keep the money and fiscal records from would-be robbers. The Commission and the architect had respect for his feelings, and Johnson got what he asked for: a 12 X 17 foot vault, ten feet high that was surrounded by eighteen-inch walls reinforced with steel. There were forty safes within the vault, each with a double combination; the access door was made of 15-inch-thick solid steel that weight 15 tons.

The court chamber is a room surrounded by white marble columns on black marble bases, and the steps leading to the dais were created from dark green Vermont marble. Above the chambers is a stained glass flanked by bronze carvings. A frieze across the top of the walls quotes Thomas Jefferson and Abraham Lincoln.

The Cornerstone

The construction of the main Capitol building took place during the worst economic depression in the nation's history. Groundbreaking took place only months after the collapse of the New York Stock Exchange. Construction, however, remained on schedule.

In keeping with tradition, a copper box containing records, documents, and other articles was placed inside the cornerstone just prior to its setting by stone masons.

The box contained the normal documents: the State Code, the Constitutions, the state directory, and a birth certificate that was drawn at random from the thirty thousand babies born in West Virginia.

The box contained other items: a copper seal used to mark safe drinking water along highways; a bottle of medicine used to treat venereal disease; a vial of typhoid vaccine; an ampule of silver nitrate; and health literature.

Present Day Complex

Today's Capitol Complex is a thing of beauty. Its architecture is still considered beautiful and inventive, and it is seated in a serene, park-like setting. Gilbert had the foresight to leave room for expansion; his plans called for impressive office buildings to be constructed around the complex.

If you visit the State Capitol today, you'll see a statue of a mountaineer carrying a rifle (one that's not military issue) and a Union flag. But on the other end of the Avenue, there's a statue of Stonewall Jackson, looking as if he is fighting a strong wind. The sculptor, it is said, tried to show Jackson symbolically "withstanding" a strong Northern wind.

From the Jackson statue, walk westward along the river to see another statue called Lincoln Walks at Midnight, depicting Abraham Lincoln in a robe.

West of the Lincoln statue is another of a marching Union soldier, added in the 1930s. This statue is unusual in that the sculptor must not have done much research on Union soldiers; they normally wore backpacks, but the statue wears a blanket roll; his musket is slung over his shoulder in a way that it could have hit the man behind him; and his cartridge box is not the style that his troops would have carried—curiously reminiscent of a story from the Civil War, in which the enemy managed to wear the right colors, but the wrong style of weapon and cartridge box!

In 1976, the state's Cultural Center was added; its design complements that of the existing structures. The center is home to the museum, library, archives, and theater, as well as many exhibits and festivals. The Cultural Center also boasts West Virginia Public Broadcasting's Mountain Stage, a 2-hour live radio show taped right in the Cultural Center Theater. The Mountain Stage Show features many nationally and internationally recognized acts who represent many venues. The show is broadcast worldwide.

If you go there...

1900 Kanawha Boulevard East
Charleston, WV 25311

304-558-4839

Guided tours are conducted Monday through Friday.

The Circus comes to town

One hundred years ago, Charleston was known as a circus town. The circus crowds gathered here, and eventually settled in the town. At that time it was known by the name "Kanawha Courthouse." One of the clowns, John Lowlow, took five minutes of his time each day to plead for the Capitol to relocate to Charleston.

John White, a resident, started his own circus in 1896. It was quite impressive; 14 wagons were required to haul his circus.

Another popular circus that was called Belford and Howard performed in West Virginia, Ohio, and Indiana; their last performance was in April, 1911. Belford and Howard featured a 12 piece band, among other entertainment; it took 100+ people to run the show.

Charleston's first courthouse was a log structure only measuring 30X 40 feet. One common myth is that records of births and/or deaths have been destroyed through a fire; however, this is not true. The courthouse did not burn down.

Colonel Thomas Bullitt

Thomas Bullitt was both a soldier and a land speculator. Originally from Prince William County, Virginia, Bullitt was a Captain during the French and Indian war. He fought alongside Colonel Washington in 1754 at the defeat in the Battle of Great Meadows. He also was defeated at the Battle of Monogahela in 1755.

By 1758, Bullitt was leading a militia company called the Forbes Expedition. They were a part of the militia commanded by James Grant. Grant's party was ambushed by the French in September of that year; Grant was captured. Bullitt rallied the troops and led a successful counterattack; eventually the French were forced to abandon the fort. When the war ended, Bullitt became adjutant general of the state militia. He also actively pursued land development.

He was sent on a mission that encompassed both of these interests in 1773, when settlers were moving into Kentucky without colonial authorization. Bullitt took 40 men and set out from the Kanawha River Valley to lay out a town site that eventually developed into the town of Louisville, Kentucky.

He discovered the salt lick that in what is now Bullitt County, KY in 1773 while surveying the land. He worked hard to maintain a peaceful relationship with the Indians.

Bullitt was deeded 1030 acres in the newly surveyed territory as a reward for his work. He looked carefully and chose a site that he thought would be a good development; today that site is downtown Charleston, West Virginia. His land lay directly on the "Great Kanawha" River by the mouth of the Elk River. He also owned another tract of land, 2,618 acres opposite St. Albans.

Thomas Bullitt sold his 1,030 acre tract of land to his brother, Judge Cuthbert Bullitt, President of the Virginia Court of Appeals. Cuthbert sold the land in 1786 to Colonel George Clendenin, a frontiersmen and soldier in General Lewis' army, who fought at the Battle of Point Pleasant in 1774. The cost of the land? "Five shillings, lawful money of Virginia."

Colonel Clendenin, his father Charles, his brothers and sister, and six other families moved to the tract of land in 1788 and built the first building within the boundaries of what is now the state capitol. The structure, known as Clendenin's Fort, was a two-story, double log building. It was said to be both bullet and arrow proof. The vast acreage was covered with elms, sycamore, and beech trees. They were thick (that's why the walls were "thick enough to stop a bullet") but remember, there were no saw mills. All the work had to be done by hand.

The first meeting of the county court took place at Clendenin's Fort on October 5, 1789. The town was chartered by the Virginia Assembly on December 19, 1794 and named Charles Town, in honor of Charles Clendenin. The town's name was shortened to Charleston to avoid confusion with two other towns in present day West Virginia that were also called Charles Town.

Downtown Historic District

At the intersection of Greenbrier Street and Kanawha Boulevard, adjacent to the Governor's Mansion, you will find Holly Grove Mansion. It was constructed in

1815 by Daniel Ruffner on what was a plantation at the time. Holly Grove is one of only three remaining homes that belonged to the Ruffner Salt Family. It is now part of the State Capitol Complex.

The East End Historical District, encompassing Kanawha Boulevard, Virginia Street, and Quarrier Street, has many homes that were built between 1890 and 1925. A great many of these homes are private residences. There are numerous styles of architecture that has been blended together in the area. You can read more about these stately homes in Chapter 7.

The Hatfields and McCoys

The Hatfields and McCoys were two families that both relocated from "old" Virginia into the Appalachian hills in the 1820s. The McCoys moved to the Kentucky wilderness, on the west side of the Tug River, while the Hatfield family made their home of the east side of the river in what is now West Virginia.

Both families lived peacefully on their own land as most pioneers did, clearing and working their land, raising the family, and so on. Both families participated in the manufacture and sale of moonshine. Both were respected and affluent, with a great deal of land holdings. The Hatfields were somewhat more politically connected than the McCoys.

Then the Civil War broke out. Since Kentucky was a Union state, the McCoys joined up with the Union, while the Hatfields were sympathetic to the

Confederate States. Two important names that came to be known for their prowess in military duty—on opposite sides—were Rand'l McCoy and Devil Anse Hatfield.

What started the feud between the two families will never really be known. There are many rumors, the most popular one being that Johnse Hatfield ran away with young Roseanne McCoy, then refused to marry her. Some say that it started because a McCoy owed a debt of one dollar to a Hatfield. Some mention the timber market. Others tell a story about Floyd Hatfield claiming a hog that really belonged to Rand'l McCoy.

The first record of violence was made in 18, and it does mention the pig; however some family members claim that the real dispute was over property lines. In either case, farming and the economy meant that both land and pigs were extremely valuable. The pig was used to prove that since it was on their land, that meant it (the land, not the pig) belonged to them. The other side disagreed. The case was taken to the Justice of the Peace, where Bill Staton testified. Bill, a relative of both the Hatfields and McCoys, caused the McCoys to lose—or so the record says, although it is noted that the case was presided over by Anderson "Preacher Anse" Hatfield. Staton was killed by Sam and Paris McCoy, but they were acquitted of the crime.

Roseanne McCoy did have an affair with Devil Anse's son, Johnse Hatfield, leaving her family to be with him in West Virginia. She returned to her family, but when she tried to go back to her lover Johnse Hatfield was kidnapped by the McCoys. Johnse married Roseanne's cousin Nancy McCoy in 1881.

In 1882, Ellison Hatfield was stabbed 26 times and then shot. It was said that he insulted Tolbert McCoy on Election Day. Subsequently, three of Roseanne McCoy's brothers (Bud, Tolbert, and Pharmer) were kidnapped, tied to Paw Paw trees, and repeatedly shot. It was said that Devil Anse Hatfield had retaliated through execution without benefit of a trial.

Some say that the violence began to ebb, but then an attorney, Perry Cline, who was related to Randolph McCoy, tried to have the murder indictments reissued. The fighting escalated. Rand'l McCoy's home was set on fire by a group of Hatfields, and as Alifair McCoy ran from the building she was shot. Eight Hatfields were kidnapped and brought to Kentucky to stand trial. Because this extradition, according to the state of West Virginia, was illegal, the United States Supreme Court became involved. The Supreme Court ruled against West Virginia and made the Hatfields stand trial in Kentucky; all eight men were found guilty. Seven received a sentence of life in prison. The last one was publicly hanged—even though hanging was illegal.

Eventually the feud claimed more than a dozen family members, which led to a call from both the Governor of Kentucky and the Governor of West Virginia to call the Militia in.

Whatever the trivial or not-so-trivial beginning, the bloody feud carried on for almost 40 years. Devil Anse Hatfield and Rand'l McCoy never reconciled; McCoy died of pneumonia in 1921 at age 86.

If you go there...

The Hatfield-McCoy Trails are a system of 500 miles of multi-use trails that cover four counties in West Virginia. The trail system has taken over ten years to create; it is now used as a demonstration project and is a public-private partnership that is held up as one of the most innovative trail systems in the country. The trails can be used for riding ATVs, motorcycles, mountain bikes, horses and hiking. See more about the Hatfield-McCoy Trails in Chapter 5, visit http://www.trailsheaven.com/ or phone 304-752-3255.

Chapter 5

Run, Walk, Hike, Ride

City Parks

Although there are plenty of sights to see and events to visit in the city of Charleston, there will be times when you want to relax and enjoy nature. We've got plenty of that to enjoy, too. For more information on any of these city parks, please call 304-348-6860.

Inside the city are several parks for picnics, walking, or just hanging out:

Cato Park is Charleston's largest municipal park. Facilities include an executive par 3 golf course with a pro shop, an Olympic-size swimming pool, and picnic areas. The park also contains tennis courts, a playground, the Garrison Nature Trail, and soccer fields. It is located on Edgewood Drive on the West Side.

Cato Golf Course – 9 holes, 3 par 4s/the rest par 3. www.cityofcharleston.org Phone 304-348-6859. 100 Baker Lane, Charleston.

The Daniel Boone Roadside Park is a historic area along Kanawha Boulevard East. The park has a boat ramp as well as a gorgeous picnic area that's just right for enjoying the scenic river view. Also at the park are the Ruffner Log Cabin and the Craik-Patton House. In December, the park is host to a holiday light show.

Haddad Riverfront Park on the 700 block of Kanawha Boulevard in downtown Charleston opened in 1995. More recently, the levee was renovated and now is an amphitheater that seats 2,500 people which is used for symphony concerts and plays. The Riverfront Park is perfect for biking, running, sunbathing, boating, or enjoying the picturesque Kanawha River.

Magic Island is located where the Elk and Kanawha Rivers join together. With a walking track and volleyball courts, it's a popular place to exercise or soak up the sunshine.

Closer to downtown, there's Laidley Field—a football, soccer, and track facility that seats 18,600. Located in the East End near the Capitol Complex, the stadium is home to many high school events, outdoor concerts, and Ribfest.

In the Appalachian Power Park, 601 Morris Street, you'll find a professional class "A" minor league baseball team, an affiliate of the Milwaukee Brewers. The park seats 4,500. The park is also home to Little League, Senior League, Big League, concerts, and festivals.

Nearby State Parks

Cabwaylingo

In the 1930's and 1940s, the Civilian Conservation Corps built camps in this heavy forest area. Their structures were log cabins with stone fireplaces. The area includes picnicking, hiking trails through more than 8,000 acres of forest, and the Tick Ridge fire tower, built in 1935. The old CCC barracks serves as a group campground.

The forest is located in Wayne County, but its name represents the counties it serves: Cabell, Wayne, Lincoln, and Mingo.

There are rustic and not-so-rustic campgrounds to accommodate every style of camping; they're open from April 1 through October 31.

The group camp is fully equipped rustic style with two barracks, a dining hall, and a shower house. The "council circle" will be perfect for your evening campfire.

Cabwaylingo holds a Forest Festival the third Saturday of each September, featuring a parade, antique car show, games, music, food and drinks.

Cabwaylingo State Forest - Route 1, Box 85, Dunlow, WV - US Route 152, 42 miles south of Huntington (turn at Missouri Branch).

Midland Trail

The James River/Kanawha Turnpike was the largest overland transportation path in the very early days of Western Virginia. The completion of the railroad, and its extensive use, all but eliminated the use of the Turnpike by the mid 1870s. The path began to be used again in the 1920s as U.S. Route 60 and is called the Midland Trail.

A newspaper article about Charleston in 1923 referred to it as the "rose city of the east," noting the large number of substantial, well-kept homes. It noted that the city lay 604 feet above sea level and occupied 6.75 square miles. The midland trail, a "great east and west highway" passed through, having already been paved to the west and, at that time, was being paved eastward from the city.

Midland Trail Scenic Highway offers more than 180 miles of scenery. It begins on the western border at the Ohio River and continues east toward Charleston. This section of the trail is called Advantage Valley. On route 60 you can see historical and cultural sights, explore many recreational activities like whitewater rafting, hiking and biking, or visit antiques, festivals, and crafts. In the center, you'll find fishing, rafting, horseback riding and rock climbing. The Midland trail winds through Fayette County and at Hico it intersects US 19. On the eastern portion, you'll find that the mountains give way to fields and limestone outcroppings. Or if you like, just soak up the scenic view. For more information call 800-458-7373 or visit www.wvmidlandtrail.com.

Civil War Trail

If you're into Civil War history, you'll be familiar with U.S. Highway 33, a northwest-southeast highway 709 miles in length that runs through Mason, Calhoun, Gilmer, Lewis, Barbour, Jackson, Roane, Randolph, Pendleton, and Upshur Counties in West Virginia.

The project of capturing Civil War History has been taken on by the state Tourism Department, the Highway Department, and the Culture and History Department, along with numerous private donors. Called the Blue and Gray trail, the route Highway 33 follows parallels that of many important battles and skirmishes that took place in West Virginia during the civil war. Many heroes and important figures are honored through the museums, monuments, and reenactments. The highway parallels the Ohio River at the northern end, then cuts through the hilly center of the state along with U.S. 119. At Weston the road becomes a 4-lane to Elkins, where it climbs into the scenic mountains. It passes near Spruce Knob, the state's highest point, and Seneca Rocks. U.S. 33 winds through Monongahela and George Washington national forests then crosses into Virginia at the Shenandoah Mountain.

Midland Trail

This trail was the path to freedom for George Washington, Daniel Boone, and many others. If you're interested in history, culture, or arts and crafts, consider following the 180-mile trail across the state.

The Midland Trail Byway leaves the Great Kanawha River at Daniel Boone Park, where it follows Kanawha Boulevard through down town and the Westside. At Pennsylvania Avenue, the Byway crosses the Elk River; Kanawha River junction and continues to follow the Kanawha. You can reach the Byway from I-64, I-77, and I-79.

Kanawha State Forest

This park is only seven miles from the center of downtown Charleston. You'll find a pool, playground, and campground, as well as plenty of picnicking and hiking, biking, and cross country skiing.

The forest encompasses 9,300 acres and provides a habitat form many birds, animal populations, and wildflowers.

The campsite has 46 sites and is fully equipped, including bathhouses and laundry facilities. There are plenty of opportunities to hunt and fish (with proper licensing, of course) as well as partaking in one of the challenging hikes or just hanging out to enjoy the scenery.

Culture and Wilderness Collide

Camp Washington Carver is an unusual mountain cultural arts center.

This camp is listed on the National Register of Historic Places. It was dedicated in 1942 as the first 4-H camp for West Virginia's African-American youth. Today, more than 10,000 people per year attend events like the African American Heritage Arts Camp and the Appalachian String Band Festival.

The camp is the state's mountain cultural arts center. Its Great Chestnut Lodge is the largest log structure of its kind in the world. Clifftop WV 304-438-3005

Trails for Riding

Hatfield-McCoy Trails – These trails boast more than 500 miles of trails covering 3,000 acres of land that are used for riding ATVs, motorcycles, mountain bikes, horses and hiking. The Trail System's director, Jeffry Lusk came on board in 2005 and began adding more trails right away—100 miles by the end of 2006. Hatfield-McCoy Trails is one of only 16 trail systems nationwide that is designated as a National Millennium Trail.

The trail system was begun in 1989; the completion should host about 2,000 miles of trails.

One of the things that makes Hatfield-McCoy a topnotch trail system is that they emphasize safety. The Hatfield-McCoy Regional Recreation Authority (HMRRA) works alongside licensed outfitters and permit vendors to stop people who might access the trails illegally, as well as stopping unlicensed trail guides from leading riders on potentially unsafe trips. They offer safety courses for riders on the trails weekends year around. The system is now allowing side-by-side UTVs (ATVs where a passenger sits by the driver) for the first time.

If you go there...

Outfitters and equipment rentals, guided tours, and packages are available. Open Year Around. Lyburn, WV (304) 752-3255 or (800) 592-2217.

Hatfield-McCoy Speedway - 4/10 mile, semi-banked clay oval track. Modifieds, Super stocks, Hot Stocks and Pure

Stocks. .6 mile north of SR 97 on US 52, then .7 mile east. Racing every Saturday night 304-664-3246

Point Pleasant

Point Pleasant is located in Mason County, which was a part of three different counties at various points in history. It was first part of Augusta County, then Greenbrier County, and in 1804 the General Assembly established what is now Mason County. It was named after a friend of George Washington's, George Mason.

Mason County grew slowly; the population in 1860 was about 9,000. The land was rich not only as farmland, but also with other resources like salt brine, clay, gravel, coal, oil, and timber.

Mason County's county seat is Point Pleasant, which is located exactly where the Kanawha River flows into the Ohio River. In 1874 the battle of Point Pleasant took place between Native Americans and colonial forces. This proved to be one of the bloodiest battles in the history of the war—the battle was considered a part of the American Revolution, in spite of the fact that it occurred six months before the war actually began. Chief Cornstalk lost 200 men and nearly 400 were wounded; the Virginians lost 81 men and 140 were wounded.

The battle did cause an important alliance to be struck between the Native Americans and their British counterparts; peace was attained throughout the first three years of the Revolutionary ward. In 1778 Chief Cornstalk was in the garrison at Point Pleasant when he was murdered (see the full story in chapter 3).

Mason County today is still picturesque, offering the visitor a beautiful view of rolling hills. In addition to the Battle Monument State Park, there is Krodel Park, 44 acres located on route 2, with a 22-acre lake offering fishing, paddle boats, and swimming; an 18 hole miniature golf course; and campsites.

Four miles outside of Point Pleasant is the West Virginia State Farm Museum, celebrating the pioneer and farming life. Visitors can see a an authentic one-room school house (circa 1870), an 1800sd log home, and a replica of the earliest Lutheran Church ever built. There is a country store, print shop, blacksmith shop, and a petting zoo.

The Chief Cornstalk Wildlife Management Area is an 11,772 acre refuge that can be reached by taking Route 35 to Nine-mile Road or by accessing Route 2 south of Gallipolis Ferry, then turning onto Crab Creek Road east. The area is about 85 percent hardwood forest and the topography is rolling to moderately steep. There is a shooting range, and t-acre fishing lake, camping sites, and plenty of hunting for deer turkey squirrel and grouse. Visitors may also obtain a special permit to trap raccoon, mink, fox, and muskrat.

Fort Randolph was the first fort at the area that is now called Point Pleasant. Built in 1774, it was destroyed only a year later and rebuilt in 1776. This is the fort where Chief Cornstalk was murdered. The fort was evacuated in 1779, possibly because of the rumor of ghosts or bad spirits, and was burned down by the Indians.

Around 1785, another fort was built on the Ohio River bank, fifty rods above the site o the old one.

In 1974, Fort Randolph was constructed to honor the American Revolution Bicentennial. It is located at Krodel Park. In 1996, a cabin, blacksmith shop, trading post, walking trail and other improvements were made to the Fort.

Point Pleasant River Museum

You will find the main focus of this museum to be on the history of river life and commercial enterprise on the Ohio and Great Kanawha rivers. Displays, video demonstrations, and special events cover the highlights topics such as great floods, boat construction, sternwheel steamers, river disasters, and the local river industry's contribution to World War II. Be sure to check the schedule for tractor pulls, art shows, the annual catfish tournament, the River of Life festival, and a Civil war re-enactment. The museum also offers a working pilot house and a research library. Hours: closed Monday; Tuesday-Friday, 10 a.m.-3 p.m. Saturday 11-4; Sunday 1-5 p.m.

www.pprivermuseum.com

Grape Hill

Confederate General John McCausland, who was educated as a mathematician and engineer, was a farmer in Mason County after the Civil war. He constructed the house at Grape Hill from thick sandstone with a metal roof. Called Grape Hill because of the abundance of wild grapes in the area, the house looks somewhat Italian in form; it included an elevator, operated by counterweights, and an ash collection system from each fireplace that drained to a bin in the basement. Next door is Maplewood Farm, which McCausland built in 1890 and passed to his son Samuel. The farm is located on U.S. Route 35 in Mason County between Charleston and Point Pleasant; it is used as a private residence.

New River Gorge

The New River flows from below Bluestone Dam at Hinton West Virginia, to just north of the U.S. Highway 19 Bridge by Fayetteville, West Virginia.

In the gorge, there is about 1,000 feet of elevation from the river bottom to the plateau. The Gorge is not only a refuge for some plant and animal species, it is also a geographical barrier that prevents other species from distributing east or west. Between 1987 and 1991 there were over thirty peregrine flacons released within the Gorge. Hundreds of species of birds inhabit the National River area and its hardwood forests, old fields, and high cliffs.

The New River Gorge cliffs are composed of very hard rock called Nutall Sandstone. The cliffs range from 20 to 150 feet in height, with numerous crags and crevices that are perfect for rock climbers. In fact, the 60,000+ acre New River Gorge National River recreation area has over 1500 routes that climbers can choose from.

The New River Gorge is sometimes referred to as "The Grand Canyon of the East". It is known not only for rock climbing, but also for its excellent fishing, and mountain biking opportunities. It is said to offer some of America's best whitewater. Rapids range from class III to class V.

The New River Gorge Park is more than 50 times longer than it is wide. It is important to allow plenty of time for visiting—and to bring an accurate map.

The New River Gorge Bridge is one of the world's largest single-arch steel span bridges. It was completed on October 22, 1977, reducing a 40 minute drive winding down narrow mountain roads to a one-minute trip across a beautiful, scenic bridge.

The bridge arches gracefully across the River, displaying the world's 2nd longest single-arch steel span. It is also the second highest bridge in the country, rising 876 feet above the New River (The Royal Gorge Bridge over the Arkansas River in Colorado is even higher.) The bridge took 3 years to build. It is 3,030 feet long and weighs 88,000,000 pounds. The cost to build it was $37,000,000.

Once a year, the New River Gorge Bridge opens for pedestrians on a day that the Fayette County Chamber of Commerce calls "bridge Day." It is always held the third Saturday in October and draws a crowd of about 250,000. Bridge Day offers organized walks, rappelling and parachuting demonstrations, vendors, and music.

The New River Gorge was extensively logged in the late 1800s and early 1900s; the landscape is improving and slowly regenerating back to its former wild state, but you can still see evidence of the logging if you look for it.

There are only fourteen rivers that are designated American Heritage Rivers in the entire United States; the New River is one of them. A "national river" is a special designation used by the Park Service that shows that the riverway contains important natural and cultural resources. The National Rivers are managed by the National park Service.

For more information: New River Gorge National River Visitor Center 304-574-2115 www.nps.gov/neri

Hawks Nest

Hawks Nest State Park consists of 276 acres on Hawks Nest Lake, an oasis of calm compared to the rushing water of the New River that forms it. Hawks Nest Lodge is located inside the park and offers 31 rooms with private balconies, many of which overlook the New River Gorge and the lake. The lodge offers a pool, tennis and game courts, a conference room, banquet rooms, and a gift shop. For information about the lodge and its accommodations, dial 1-800-CALL-WVA and ask for Hawks Nest.

Above the main overlook you will find a rustic log building that was built by the Civilian Conservation Corps in the early 1930s. This building is now a museum, displaying artifacts from Indian and pioneer days. Admission is free, and the hours will vary but it is open from April 1 through November 1.

If you'd like to take a trip from the Hawks Nest lodge to the marina at the bottom of the New River Gorge, consider the tramway. Its schedule is:

Saturday and Sunday only, May through Memorial Day;

Daily, Memorial Day through Labor Day;

Saturday and Sunday, Labor Day through September;

Daily Oct. 1 through the last weekend in October.

The hours are:

Weekdays, 11 a.m. to 4:45 p.m. Closed Mondays.

Weekends, 11 a.m. to 6:45 p.m.

Water Adventures on the New and Gauley Rivers:

Mountain River Tours – These tours, over 30 years in the making, cater to convention groups. They offer one to three hour rafting trips, including half-day, full-day, and special scenic float trips for seniors. Various white-water trips are available on both the New and Gauley rivers. P.O. Box 88, Sunday Road, Hico, WV 25854. 304/658-5266, 1-800-822-1386 http://www.raftmrt.com/

New and Gauley River Adventures - River vacations as well as river-related adventures for travelers of all ages and levels of experience. P.O. Box 44, Lansing Road, Lansing, WV 25862. 304/574-3008 or 1-800-SKY-RAFT.

Ace Adventure Center – White water rafting on the New River Gorge and Gauley River. Also offers guided rock climbing, caving, horse back rides, and instructional Kayak clinics. Located in Oak Hill, West Virginia. Phone 888-ACE-RAFT.

New River Jet Boats

Board a jet boat at Hawks Nest State Park and ride to the New River Gorge Bridge. 304-469-2525 www.newriverjetboats.com

North American River Runners

NARR offers Whitewater rafting on the New and Gauley Rivers, as well as catered meals. They offer a campground and a complete whitewater paddling shop. They have more than twenty-five years of experience on the river and offer both a brochure and video. US Rt. 60, Hico, WV 25854-0081. Located on Route 61 1/4 mile west of US 19. 800-950-2585. www.narr.com

Rivers Resort offers whitewater rafting on the New, Gauley and Cheat rivers. Choose from one and two day trips that include such activities as family float, fishing trips, llama trekking and kayaking. There are also camping and RV hook-ups available. Fayette Station Road Fayette

304/574-3834. http://www.riversresort.com/

Songer Whitewater offers climbing trips for beginners (4 hour climbing and rappelling course), basic rock climbing, and climbs for the more experienced. Visitors ride on a pontoon boat to the climbing area. Or if you prefer, enjoy whitewater rafting, horseback riding, mountain biking or bass fishing. Rt 19 at Miller Ridge Rd. Fayetteville 1-800-356-RAFT.

www.songerwhitewater.com

Whitewater- a full "adventure resort" with a restaurant and its own hiking and biking trails. 800-545-RAFT www.goraftingwv.com

Horseback Riding

New River Trail Rides

Choose from either hourly or overnight guided horseback rides and wagon rides.

Wonderland Rd. Oak Hill 304/465-4819 or 1-888-743-3982.

www.ridewva.com

Burning Springs

The following is a part of the property distribution portion of George Washington's will; this section was labeled simply "Great Kanawha."

Near the Mouth West	10990		
East side above	7276		
Mouth of Cole River	2000		
Opposite thereto	2950		
Burning Spring	125		
	23341 [acres]		[$] 200,000 (k)

(k) These tracts are situated on the Great Kanawha River, and the first four are bounded thereby for more than forty miles. It is acknowledged by all who have seen them (and of the tract containing 10990 acres which I have been on myself, I can assert) that there is no richer, or more valuable land in all that Region; They are conditionally sold for the sum mentioned in the Schedule—that is $200,000 and if the terms of that Sale are not complied with they will command considerably more. The tract of which the 125 acres is a Moiety, was taken up by General Andrew Lewis and myself for, and on account of a bituminous Spring which it contains, of so inflammable a nature as to burn as freely as Spirits, and is as nearly difficult to extinguish.

Washington acquired 250 acres in 1771 in what is now West Virginia; he bought it specifically because it contained an oil and gas spring. By 1819, the first major wells were drilled at Petroleum, West Virginia (outside Parkersburg). In 1860 they were drilled at Burning Springs. Oil then sold for $30 per barrel, which would be about $2,000 in today's market; and a natural gusher could be drilled at only 100 feet; so there were numerous oil men–turned-politicians who had made a fortune at Burning springs in 1860-61.

On May 9, 18632, the Burning Springs oil field was destroyed by General Jones and Confederate troops.

If you go there…

Burning Springs is located seven miles from Elizabeth on Route 5 in Wirt County, which is called the Little Kanawha Scenic Byway. The park there consists of 31 acres, 1800 feet of riverfront, a museum, an operating antique oil derrick, and much more.

Don't miss the Oil and Gas Museum in Parkersburg, which serves as an anchor site to celebrate the oil industry and the Civil War. It is located at 119 Third Street,

Parkersburg. Phone 304-485-5446. Hours are Weekdays 11-4, Saturday 11-5, and Sunday 12-5.

Websites

These are some websites that outdoor enthusiasts may find helpful during their visit to Charleston, West Virginia:

trailsheaven.com

wvbyways.com

wvescapes.com

wvforestry.com

wvparks.com

wvriversports.com

wvstateparks.com

wvtrails.com

mountainstatewheelers.org

westvirginiaski.com

wvwintersports.com

iplayoutside.com

crcyclists.org

Racing and Tracks

Rolling Thunder Extreme Race Park offers both a 300′ dirt and sand ATV drag strip track and an asphalt oval track for stock and go-kart racing. There is ATV drag racing every Saturday night as well as concessions and a bandstand. From Route 119, take the Logan exit to Rte 10 East. Follow Rt 10 east to 3-mile curve. Track is on the right 304-855-7425

Wild and Wonderful WV Off-Road Championship Series

This series features a 3-5 mile, off-road course for motorcycles and quads. Phone 304-864-6908 www.kootnzadventures.com

Skate Park
Outdoor Extremes
Full indoor skate park.
3716 MacCorkle Ave., SE, Charleston.
304-925-8463.

Amusement Parks

Camden Park was originally a picnic area created by the Camden Interstate Railway, a streetcar system in 1903. Parks like this were common near the streetcars to help boost weekend and holiday traffic. Camden has hosted baseball games, fairs, and hundreds of other attractions over the years. Although the era of the streetcar is long gone, the Park is now a traditional amusement park. Enjoy the carousel, Dodge-'em cars, Log Flume or the Big Dipper, games or enjoy a snack from one of many vendors.

WaterWays Waterpark

This full-service water park features slides, a pool, kiddie pool, go-karts, mini-golf, an archery range, walking trails and picnic shelters. Located on US 119 in Julian, 20 minutes south of Charleston. Phone 304-369-6125 or visit the website at www.waterwayspark.com

For more information.

Waves of Fun
304-562-0518
Water park, Mini-golf and Sand Volleyball
I-64, exit 34 - Hurricane, Valley Park Dr.
Memorial Day to Labor Day

Chapter 6

Fires and Firefighting in Charleston

In the 1800s, "firefighting" generally consisted of a disorganized form of a bucket brigade. Citizens were happy to participate, since buildings were usually situated close together, so a fire in one area could quickly spread to other buildings. Charleston's first record of having an official fire fighting team was in 1845. At that time, equipment consisted of a two-hand pump engine that was pulled by the men wherever it was needed. Firemen were called into action via the use of a metal triangle that was struck by a heavy hammer; this hung by the academy building on Quarrier Street. If anyone saw a fire they would run to the headquarters and strike the triangle repeatedly with the hammer. The firemen would go to the fire house, grab the ropes that were attached to the pump wagon, and drag the wagon to the water source, often the river or a well. Climbing onto the wagon, they would pump the water onto the fire.

The Charleston area, like many other cities, experienced numerous fires in the late 1800s/early 1900s. Typically, buildings were cheaply built frame structures. There was no building code or construction regulation. There were two different capitol buildings that were destroyed by fire. The first one in 1921 happened on January 3. The Capitol building had served for 36 years, since the capital moved from Wheeling in 1885. Some ammunition had been stored on the top floor of the building by the state police, along with machine guns and rifles. The ammunition was set off by the fire and exploded; smoke could be seen from miles away. While the firefighters were busy working the fire, two men stole one of the fire trucks and took it for a ride around Charleston. They were arrested.

The Hale House, Charleston's luxurious railroad hotel, burned in 1885. Located where a parking lot is now at Hale Street and Kanawha Boulevard, after the fire the Ruffner hotel was built in its place. The Ruffner, an impressive 7-story structure with 200 guest rooms, had its own ferry that carried passengers from the C&O railroad station across the Kanawha River. The hotel remained active until 1970 when it was torn down.

In 1874 a blaze that became known as The Great Fire destroyed the entire "business block"; all the buildings on both sides of Kanawha Street between Court and Alderson Street.

A 1930s writer gave the following description told of the firefighting in the 1870s: "...there was a fire station at the corner of Lee and Brooks Street, 53 years ago. The firemen used small fire reels that they pulled by hand."

Charleston's very first horse-drawn fire engine, a Silsby, was purchased for the city by Mayor John Hale.

It would have been impossible to pull by hand as the men had been previously doing—it weighted between 3 and 4 tons. It was 1901 before motorized equipment began to be the norm.

In order to better prepare for fighting the inevitable fires, hydrants, which were really cisterns were built in the town in 1886. Those were for fires that were away from the river. For those that were close, the hose was taken to the river and water suctioned up from there. Fire hoses had been invented earlier in the 1800s; the first hoses were stitched together for their entire length, so they were extremely leaky. Later leather hoses were put into use. Horse drawn wagons were used to carry the hoses to the scene. The use of horses drawn wagons continued until 1923.

Courthouse Explosion

One of the most spectacular fires took place in 1905 at the courthouse, as the result of an explosion. Colonel George Patton, Attorney, Montgomery Saunders, Chief Deputy County Clerk, Judge Green, Elmer Harless (deputy clerk), and Mary Poindexter and Fannie Gardner (clerks) were all injured in the explosion.

It is said that escaping natural gas used in the vault of the office of the county clerk at the courthouse exploded, with the most serious and perhaps fatal results to two of the best known citizens of Charleston.

The vault was very dark, so it was customary for one to light a match upon entering, using that to ignite a gas jet that was supplied with natural gas. Deputy Clerk Saunders went to enter the vault and struck a match... almost instantly a terrific explosion followed. Colonel Patton, standing beside him, was thrown clear out of the vault door, his forehead striking against the door frame. When he fell his clothing was ablaze, and his hair and mustache entirely burned off. Deputy Harless rushed to his assistance and was burned on the hand. Harless tore off Patton's clothes and extinguished him. Montgomery Saunders was knocked down by the force of the explosion and had to be dragged out. Saunders died as a result of his injuries; Patton lingered but suffered lasting effects from the explosion.

Most of the fires were like that of the Pasteboard Capitol in 1927; an article dated March 3, 1927 in the Charleston Gazette told of the fire "Of uncertain origin, spreading almost instantaneously through...within a half an hour."

This fire started on the second story or the roof. This ways typical of the fires of the day; no one knew how they started, and they destroyed entire buildings almost instantly.

It was later determined that the fire plug located at the intersection of Capitol and Washington Street (and therefore, at the fire department) was "dead." One of the fire trucks that responded to the blaze also went out of commission as soon as it arrived, and had to be pushed away from the fire.

A child approached the blaze and got too close. He caught his coat on fire, and firemen turned a hose on him full force, driving him a full 20 feet on the end of the stream, but saving his life.

Fire House of the Early Days

By 1930 the city's fire department had grown to 10 companies that owned about $300,000 in equipment. The fire department at that time was more like a social club, with gaudy uniforms (according to the citizens of Charleston) that included red flannel shirts with black velvet trim and black fire hats. Their "club" had by-laws and a system of fines and assessments that could be made against association members; five black balls required the resignation of the member.

If members missed a fire, they were fined 25 cents; missing a meeting invoked a fine of 10 cents for members and 25 cents for the president or vice president.

In the '30s, water was hard to find for fighting fires. The steam engines used cisterns, but they only held about 100 barrels—not much for a large structure blaze. They were filled with water that was hauled up from the river in water carts.

In most areas, firefighters who served at least 10 years could be exempt from sitting on juries or going into military service. One important change occurred in 1932, when the state law mandated that fire officers were civil service employees; prior to that the officers were always appointed by the Mayor of Charleston.

Seven Firemen Lost

In 1949 the Woolworth's Five and Dime on Capitol Street caught fire in the wee hours of the morning. A policeman noticed the fire and called it in; by the time firefighters arrived, the basement and first floor were engulfed in flame. The firemen decided to cut a hole in the wooden floor in order to spray water into the basement. The floor gave way and seven firefighters plunged to their death into the basement. In addition to the seven who were killed 13 firemen were injured, and the damage was said to have cost over $1 million. Today the office building at 205 Capitol Street is said to have ghosts of the firefighters walking the halls.

Fire Destroys Baseball Stadium

Charleston's baseball history began in 1910 with the Statesmen (later the Senators) a class D team. Baseball was sporadic for the first 20 years of its existence here. The Senators returned to Charleston as part of the Class C Mid-Atlantic league in 1931. They competed for 12 seasons using Kanawha Park as their home field. In 1943, a fire destroyed almost all of their grandstands there; the team was forced to play most of its games away from Charleston fans.

For the next 5 years, Charleston had no professional baseball team; then Watt Powell and a $350,000 government bond helped to build the Watt Powell Park in the same Kanawha City location. The stadium held over 4,000 people, but many chose to watch the games from the nearby railroad line instead.

The park closed in 2005 when the new Appalachian Power Park was constructed. The current team, West Virginia Power, http://wvpower.com, is a class "A" Milwaukee Brewers affiliate.

Chapter 7

Architecture

If you'd like to take a glimpse into the life of the early 20th century, downtown Charleston is the place to do it. The revitalization efforts, unlike those of most modern cities, have honored the rich history and the amazing architecture that exists in Charleston. Capitol Street, which was once the bustling business center, is lined with quaint shops and businesses. Davis Square and the Kanawha Public Library are just two examples of a style of building that represents an era long past.

In 1991, the Charleston Downtown historic district was added to the National Register of Historic Places. It is roughly bounded by broad street, the Kanawha River, summers Street, the Conrail railroad tracks. It encompasses 989 acres and 177 buildings.

In 1996 the Clendenin historic district was added: bounded by First Avenue and Kanawha Ave between 5th and French Streets, covering 200 acres and thirty-seven buildings; colonial revival, classical revival, and late gothic revival architecture are some of the examples of the architecture you can see there.

All totaled, 13 areas of Kanawha County have been added to Nation Register of Historic Places.

West Virginia's Capitol

Although the Capitol building and its design were extensively covered in Chapter 4, there are a few items of interest that should be noted here.

The Capitol building has been deemed one of the greatest state capitol buildings in the United States. They received this designation in 1994 from a group that certainly knows their way around large office buildings—the Building Owners and Managers Association International.

The Capitol building houses hundreds of lawmakers, employees, and visitors in its 535,000+ square feet of hallways. The busy people within may not notice all the intricate detailing in its design as they go about their daily business. The Capitol building contains seven different kinds of marble and is insured for $200 million.

Roman Corinthian colonnades support a vaulted ceiling which, if one cares to look up, contains carved plaster rosettes that "grow" from the ceiling. They're supposed to represent the state tree, the Sugar Maple, and two other popular local trees, the Magnolia and the Red oak.

Even the lighting has historical significance; in the hallways leading to the Senate and the House of Delegates you can find 55 black and gold Belgian marble columns, each topped by alabaster sconce lights—representing each of the state's 55 counties.

The House and Senate wings each feature different styles, but they both sport chandeliers that are said to be worth $500,000. The chandelier in the center of the Rotunda is even bigger; it weights 4,000 pounds and takes 96 light bulbs. Cleaning it requires carefully removing each separate crystal for dipping into a special cleanser.

Looking at the outside view, if West Virginia's Capitol dome seems tall to you—it is. It's 4 ½ feet taller than the Washington, D.C. capitol building.

Governor's Mansion

Located on the grounds of the Capitol Complex is the Governor's Mansion, which was designed by Charleston architect Walter F. Martens and constructed in 1924. The 30-room executive mansion is built in a traditional Georgian colonial style. It blends perfectly with the other buildings in the Capitol Complex with its air of quiet dignity. The ground floor contains state rooms decorated with exquisite period antiques; the second floor is the governor's private residence. Tours are conducted on Thursday and Friday between 9:30 am-11:30 am. For more information please call 304-558-4839.

Holly Grove

Directly beside the Governor's Mansion on the Capitol Complex is Holly Grove Mansion, which was built in 1815 on what was at the time a plantation located east of Charleston. Daniel Ruffner constructed Holly Grove; it's one of three remaining buildings from the Ruffner salt family. Holly Grove is maintained as part of the state Capitol Complex. It was said that Henry Clay, Andrew Jackson, and others were entertained at Holly Grove. Wise marched his troops directly past it in 1861, when the first Confederate troops came into the Kanawha Valley and down the river to confront the Federals in the Battle of Scary Creek.

The 192-year-old Holly Grove has been vacant since 2004. It is preserved within the State Capitol Complex. The 2007 plan for restoring the home contains an estimate of about $3.8 million.

Touring Charleston's Historic Homes

Craik-Patton House

The Craik-Patton House is listed on the National Register of Historic Places. It was built by James Craik in 1834 and was first called "Elm Grove." Craik had inherited land near Charleston from his grandfather, Dr. James Craik, the first surgeon general of the Continental army, who was a close friend of George Washington. Mr. Craik was first a lawyer and farmer, but became a rector in the Episcopal Church. He and Mrs. Craik and their seven children resided in the house, which is done in a beautiful American Greek Revival style. It was one of the first clapboard frame houses in the area.

In 1846 Mr. Craik was called to pastor a church in Louisville, Kentucky. The house in Charleston was sold to

Isaac Reed, who sold it to George Smith Patton for $2,900 in 1858. Patton came to Charleston to practice law, but then the war broke out and he put his VMI education to use. George S. Patton was the Colonel who led the Kanawha Riflemen, the outfit that later became part of the 22nd Virginia Infantry in the Confederate Army. Patton died at the 3rd Battle of Winchester, Virginia, in 1864. Colonel Patton was also the grandfather of the well-known General George S. Patton.

The Craik-Patton house was originally built on Virginia Street; it was later moved to Lee Street. In the 1970s, the National Society of the Colonial Dames of America purchased the home and moved it again, this time to Daniel Boone Park on Kanawha Boulevard East where it sits today. It is furnished in the way it might have been in 1834, with the exception of one room which is furnished in a later style in honor of George Smith Patton. Tours are available of the house, herb garden, and boxwood gardens and the Ruffner log cabin, which is also situated on the grounds. 2809 Kanawha Boulevard East; Located in the Daniel Boone Park on Highway 60 at the Eastern City Limit. For more information call 304-925-5341 Open: Mid-April through September, Tuesday-Thursday: 10:00 a.m. to 4:00 p.m. or by appointment. The house also has a refurbished meeting room which can accommodate up to 50 for meetings and other functions.

McFarland-Ruby House

In 1836, the McFarland-Ruby house (then called the Hubbard House) was built by brothers Norris and

William Whitteker. Designed in the classical revival style, the house is a two-story brick featuring four Doric columns and a triangular pediment. Strangely, it is one of few historic Southern homes without a name. Henry McFarland was its first owner, purchasing it directly from the builders just a few days before he was married.

The house next belonged to the Ruby family, successful Charleston business owners, who vacated it during the Civil War. It served as housing for wounded Civil War soldiers for a period of time, and was struck by a cannonball in 1862. The Rubys returned to the area after the war, selling the house to J.W. Crowley in 1922. Crowley added most of the modern conveniences that exist there, including installing electricity.

It has been called Hubbard House during the latter portion of its 170+ years; that's because Elizabeth Hubbard's family owned it from 1941 until her passing in 1997. Ms. Hubbard wanted the home to continue to serve as a residence, so she left it to Charleston's First Presbyterian Church upon her death.

The house has been carefully restored using photographs from about 1910, which seem to be the earliest ones available. A jug of wine is said to have been found in a secret compartment in the house. Alcohol was outlawed in the 1920s, and the newspaper found with the jug was dated then; so the theory is that the compartment was designed for the homeowner's secret stash of illegal alcohol. Ironically, the newspaper that was wrapped around the jug contained a front page story about a bootleg investigation. It is believed that Elizabeth Hubbard did not know about the secret compartment.

The first floor is now used for exhibits, programs, and meetings; the second floor houses the Humanities Council offices. The carriage house was also restored and is used for meeting space. Located at 1310 Kanawha Boulevard, Charleston. 304-346-8500.

Littlepage Stone Mansion

Littlepage is one of only six properties in Charleston from the pre-Civil war era. The Stone Mansion is a two-story Federal-style residence that was built in 1845. The blocks that it was constructed from are ashlar, a smooth, square-cut type of stone. The mansion is now a part of the Charleston Housing Authority, which in 2003 spent over $300,000 on renovations to the building; it is open only by appointment. Call Charleston Housing Authority, Washington Street, West, at Rebecca Street.

Old Stone House

This house is one of the oldest existing structures in Charleston today. It was built by Samuel Shrewsbury in 1810. Samuel and his brother John came here from Bath County, VA and settled in Belle. They married the daughters of Virginia Colonel John Dickinson; Dickinson subsequently deeded them 704 acres of Kanawha Salines land—causing the Dickinson-Shrewsbury heirs to become a powerhouse in the salt industry.

The Shrewsbury property originally extended west to Burning Springs and east to Witcher Creek Bridge.

The house is built in a style that is now referred to as Trans-Allegheny pioneer architecture; the walls are 18 inches thick and were rubble (randomly placed stones that are stacked and fitted together) with sandstone quoins at the corners, much like many old English structures. The hand-cut sandstone was gathered from the hillside nearby. A nearby walnut grove supplied ample wood for the interior walls, cupboards, and magnificent woodwork, all of which were hand hewn. The 3-story home was occupied continuously; it served as a stagecoach inn for some years. In 1985, the Belle Historical Restoration Society, Inc. purchased and carefully refurbished it.

To get there, take U.S. Route 60 East to Belle Exit, then go 1/2 mile east on DuPont Avenue and turn right on Stubb Drive. Open from the third Saturday in May to October. For more information phone 949-3289.

Sam Starks House

Sam Starks was a nationally known African-American leader who was a Charleston native. Among his many accomplishments was his appointment as the first black state librarian in the U.S. 413 Shrewsbury Street, between 1000 block of Washington Street and Lewis Street.

Former Governor's Mansion

Prior to 1923, the Governor of West Virginia lived in a large Queen Anne-style house.

Victorian block, Capitol Street

This group of buildings includes some of the oldest structures on Capitol Street, dating back to 1887. It is located on the east side of Capitol Street between Virginia and Quarrier Streets.

Davis Park

An immaculate expanse of greenery that connects Capitol and Summers Streets, the park contains an equestrian statue of Henry G. Davis, who was a U.S. Senator from West Virginia during 1871-83. Davis was also a railroad man and a vice presidential candidate. He is also honored with a copy of this statue in Elkins, West Virginia. Located at Capitol and Lee Streets.

First Presbyterian Church is a spectacular example of early 1900s architecture; designed by Weaver, Werner, and Atkins, the beauty and intricacy of the exterior is only surpassed by the domed arch on the interior which serves to enhance the ambience of the sanctuary, complete with a full-size pipe organ that is used every week for services. The Church is located one block off Kanawha Boulevard at the corner of Virginia Street and Leon Sullivan Way; 16 Leon Sullivan Way. Open daily from 8 a.m. to 4 p.m.

Kanawha Presbyterian Church

Reverend Henry Ruffner established the Presbyterian ministry in Charleston in 1815; his work was carried on by his son, David Ruffner, who is often referred to as "the Father of Presbyterianism in the Kanawha Valley."This church was designed by Edwin Anderson, architect. Its cornerstone was laid on April 20, 1873, and the church was was built over a period of years from 1873 to 1885. That's because an economic hardship struck the area in the late 70s; in fact, the basement foundation stood only partially framed in, so children were able to skate on the ice that formed on the standing water in the basement. The church was completed by 1885, and the roster quickly grew to over 200 members.

It is Charleston's oldest extant house of worship, and stands as a significant example of High Victorian Gothic architecture. The eight stained glass windows depict pictures of Christ as well as pictures of the church's own history.

You can visit the church at 1009 Virginia Street, East.

East end historical district

Listed on the National Register of Historic Places since 1983, this area remains charmingly well-preserved. The buildings here are maintained true to their period architecture, which mostly ranges between 1895-1925, and styles are eclectic: Greek Revival, Queen Anne, Colonial, Georgian and Italianate. The East End is an excellent neighborhood for a walking tour. Bradford and East at Kanawha.

Breezemont

Built in 1905, Breezemont was a private mansion built by General Cornelius Watts. Watts was an attorney, and a former state attorney general and senator. It is located at 915 Breezemont Drive and is maintained as a private residence. It is said that there is still a portrait of Watts hanging inside the home.

Sunrise Mansion

Sunrise, a stately 36-room Georgian mansion, was built on 16 acres of Woodland in 1905 by then-Governor William A. MacCorkle.

MacCorkle was actually a Democrat who supported the Confederate tradition, but he was not a bitter politician. He served both in the State Senate and as governor from 1892-1896. He also was the author of several historical books.

MacCorkle intended for his home to be well-visited, and it was; some of the visitors included Adlai Stevenson, boxer James Corbett, composer John Philip Sousa, and evangelist Billy Sunday.

In 1961 the mansion was purchased by a nonprofit organization, who created a foundation opened the house to the public for free admission. It was then used as a museum for about 40 years. After the Clay Center for the Arts opened in downtown Charleston, the Sunrise museum was closed and the house sold to a private party. The new owners have lovingly restored the home and it is now maintained as a private law office. Located at 746 Myrtle Street.

Capitol Center Theatre

This theater originally opened in 1914 as a vaudeville venue, and later transformed into a movie theatre. The West Virginia Capitol Theatre is one of Charleston's leading entertainment spots. It was restored and re-opened as the Capitol Center in 1984. part of West Virginia State University, this historical landmark never ceases to entertain. 123 Summers Street.

405 Capitol Street (1929) This site was formerly the Daniel Boone Hotel, one of Charleston's most lavish hotels, built by a progressive group of Charleston citizens at a cost of more than $1.2 million. It was named for Daniel Boone, the frontiersman who resided for a time in Kanawha County. This building has housed such notable guests as John F. Kennedy, Bob Hope, Tyrone Power and Elvis Presley. The interior was recently renovated in a unique style for office space while maintaining the original style and charm of the exterior. It is now known for its 10-story atrium. 405 Capitol Street.

C & O Railroad Depot (1905)

The brick and terra cotta trimmed depot gave the state capital with a grand point of interest once upon a time. It was completely refurbished inside and out in 1987, restoring it to its original grandeur; a companion building in much the same style was built directly beside it. The old depot houses a restaurant on the main level with office space on the upper level. It also still houses the local depot for AMTRAK.

The Woolworth building was a fine example of architecture even in its day; it was written up in the New York Times in 1911. The building was destroyed by fire in 1949, in a blaze that killed seven local firemen (see chapter 6 for the full story). The structure was subsequently rebuilt. There is now a plaque commemorating the fallen firefighters at the office building, located at 205 Capitol Street.

Sunrise Carriage Trail

Sunrise Carriage Trail is located adjacent to the Sunrise mansion. The trail is a meandering 15-foot-wide path that gently zigzags back and forth for about .65 miles through a lush landscape of woodlands, wildflowers, and ornamental plantings. In addition to the native flora, visitors will see beautiful historical stone works, some only remnants, and massive benches. The path descends about 180 feet from the top to the bottom.

The Carriage Trail was originally used to travel from Sunrise to downtown Charleston; William MacCorkle found that the steep public road, which is now Bridge Road, was difficult to use for hauling construction materials—massive stones that were being hauled by teams of oxen—to build his estate. So he purchased the adjacent acreage that is now the Carriage trail from a landowner and built a private access road that had a gentler slope. Following the construction, the governor continued to use his private trail for carriage transportation in and out of the city.

There are two monuments located on the Trail. The first was put there to commemorate two women who were buried on the Trail and were accidentally disinterred during construction. When MacCorkle reburied them, he had no idea who they were. So he consulted with Captain John Slack, a former Union soldier and historian, who told him that the two women had been captured along the Kanawha river in 1862 by Confederate forces and were shot after it was determined that they were Union spies. However, another former Union soldier later confessed that he was actually a part of the firing squad that executed the two women.

It is now believed that Governor MacCorkle and John Slack actually knew who the women were, as they were from Charleston, but the men decided to keep the information a secret. So the women are commemorated on the Carriage Trail, but their identities remain a mystery.

The other monument on the bend near the Upper part of the trail has an inscription at the base that reads: IN LOVING MEMORY OF ISABELLE MacCorkle. The governor and his beloved daughter Isabelle were involved in a vehicle crash on route 60 in 1926, and she died the next day at the age of 35. He erected the shrine soon afterward on a secluded section of the Trail.

For more information, phone 304-342-7676.

Other Interesting Architecture

Kanawha county courthouse

The main section of the Kanawha County Courthouse was built as a picturesque Roman-style structure in 1892. The next section, a "boulevard unit" was added in 1917. The Virginia Street addition was then added in 1924. A more modern courthouse annex was constructed across Virginia Street in 1985. 409 Virginia Street, East.

Kanawha Public Library

This building was originally the Federal Court Building and the Charleston Post Office. It re-opened as the public library in 1966. The outside of the structure is a classical facade set off by a colonnade of ionic columns. The fountain sculpture was created in 1966 by Robert Cronback of New York. 123 Capitol Street.

The Loewenstein building

This building was constructed in 1900, and was originally the Loewenstein & Sons Hardware and Saddle Firm. Recently the interior has been renovated for use as offices and apartments. The exterior of the pressed brick building exhibits eclectic late Victorian and classical detailing featuring Jack Arches and Keystones above the windows and on the upper floors. 233 Capitol Street.

The Masonic building

This unique building was constructed in 1915 by architect H. Rus Warne. Its many features include Gothic pinnacles, pointed arches and window tracery all done in terra cotta detailing. 107 Hale Street.

Laidley-Summers Glenwood Estate (Marshall University)

Glenwood Estate was built by the Laidleys in 1852 on an estate of 366 acres in what is now the much more urban Edgewood section of Charleston's West Side. It was later owned by the Summers family and then the Quarrier family, some of Charleston's most prominent early families. Glenwood was given to the graduate college foundation by Lucy Quarrier. It is listed on the National Register of Historic Places.

The structure continues to be one of the state's finest examples of classical Greek Revival architecture. The main house and outbuildings have been restored and are surrounded by spacious perennial, herb, and boxwood gardens. Glenwood is used by the University for functions such as lectures, recitals, and other educational programming. 800 Orchard Street West Washington Street to Park Avenue. Turn right on Park, left on Orchard, and the house in on the right. Hours are 9 am to 10 pm Monday through Saturday. 304-346-5525

Wayne Cottage

The Wayne Cottage was the original name for a home that is now known as The Alma Lee. It was the home of Minnie Wayne Cooper, an African-American teacher who was a favorite of Booker T. Washington. She was also a civic leader; she helped integrate Kanawha County Schools without incident in the 1960s. Governor John D.

Rockefeller IV awarded her the first state Washington-CarverAwardforheracclaimed,lifelongcivicleadership. The property was originally conveyed to Mrs. Cooper's parents by the Dickinson family. The Wayne family helped organize the African Zion Baptist Church. Mrs. Cooper's mother was Martha Sullivan Wayne.

Mrs. Cooper lived in her 4 room cottage for 82 years until 1989. The 4 room cottage was reconstructed in 1998 into a 2 story home, and the original cottage bricks were used to build the fireplace in Booker's Cabin.

Spring Hill Cemetery, Charleston

Spring Hill Cemetery was begun in 1870, after the municipal cemetery by the Kanawha River ran out of space. Spring Hill was designed by A.J. Vosburg with rambling geometric patterns for walkways. Its location is one of the Valley's most beautiful sites. Now over 130 years old, it covers more than 150 acres and has over 80,000 lots, many of them belonging to founding fathers, governors, and other people important to Charleston's History.

General Appleton, an officer of a famous black regiment during the Civil War rests here, as does Thomas Brown who sold General Robert E. Lee his horse, Traveler. There are many notable Charleston names: Ruffner, Quarrier, Dickinson, Laidley, and Summers. There is also a different cemetery that is called Spring Hill located in Huntington.

Bird walks are held at Spring Hill Cemetery Park on Sunday mornings during peak migration seasons. To participate, meet at the parking lot on Middleton Drive below the Mausoleum at 8:00 am. Spring Hill Cemetery Park can be reached from the North end of Morris Street by going right on Piedmont Road and up the ramp over the interstate, then on up to the top of the hill on Farnsworth Drive. Open Monday through Friday 7:30 a.m. to 4:00 p.m. Gates are open dawn to dusk every day.

Hale House

An 1838 2-story brick house, Hale House is now the home to Cabin Creek Quilts. Located in Malden, the house was built by Dr. John Hale. He was the great grandson of Mary Ingles and came to Malden in order to practice medicine, but instead became one of the early salt makers and then a Charleston hotel entrepreneur. He also wrote an important history book called TransAllegheny Pioneers, about Mary Ingles' famous trek home and spanning key historical events of the local area.

Cabin Creek Quilts was begun in 1970 by James Thibeault. Employing around 100 quilt makers, CCQ is unique in that its seamstresses all work from their homes. Quilts have been made for U.S. Presidents and numerous celebrities. After restoring the Hale House in 1991, the CCQ has become a leader in promoting Malden History and tourism. In 1994 they restored Norton House as a training center for CCQ; it also serves as a community center when needed for meetings, and it is home to the Midland Trail Scenic Highway Association. Video tapes of historical nature or walking tours are shown on the property. All of the CCQ interests are located at 4208 Malden Drive.

Another Hale House was built by Dr. Hale in Charleston; he became the mayor suddenly, in 1871, after the death of Mayor Henry C. Dickinson. Dickinson was a Confederate war hero, he came from the Malden salt family of Dickinsons, and he was one of the founders of Kanawha Valley Bank. Hale built Hale House at Hale Street and Kanawha Boulevard within the year.

This Hale House was used as an elegant railroad hotel in its early days. The C&O railroad was completed across the river, on the south side. The station was located where the Charleston station currently stands. The river had no bridge at that time, so a ferry was used for moving passengers across the river from the hotel to the railroad station and back.

Midland Trail

The Midland Trail/ U.S. Route 60 extends across West Virginia over 180 miles, through a total of 41 towns. There are many attractions along the trail to suit every interest: arts, crafts, culture, Civil War History, historical homes, museums, fishing, boating, hiking, rock climbing, and much more. The following is a list of some of the historic homes and other sites that are located near the Charleston area on the Midland Trail:

- Huntington

♦ **Coin Harvey House – Huntington, W.Va.**

1305 Third Avenue

Constructed in 1874 by William Hope Harvey, the "Coin" Harvey Residence is often considered one of the city's loveliest houses. William "Coin" Harvey was a gifted economist who is most remembered for his theory calling for the free coinage of silver. He also ran for president of the United States in 1932 as a third party candidate. The stucco house is designed along classical lines with Italianate detailing. The construction date of 1874 is carved into the façade's center.

MuseumofRadioandTechnology,ClassicCarsAutomotive Museum, Heritage Farm Museum and Village,

Huntington Museum of Art

Barboursville

Toll House

Milton

Union Baptist Church, Morris Convalescent Nursing Home,

Yesterday's Memories, Blenko Glass Museum

Hurricane

Plantation Corner, Main Street Gallery, Museum in the Community, Caboose Museum

♦ St. Albans

St. Marks Episcopal Church, Turner/Callihan House, Historic Sidewalk Tour

- Malden

  Booker T. Washington's Cabin, Hale House, Norton House

- Belle

  Old Stone House

- Cedar Grove

  Virginia's Chapel

  This chapel was constructed as a graduation gift from salt magnate William Tompkins for his oldest daughter, Virginia. M. Homer Cummings wrote a song about it in 1948 entitled "The Old Brick Church by the Side of the Road," which is memorialized in The Methodist Hymnal. The chapel is located near the Tompkins Mansion, Cedar Grove.

- Glen Ferris

  Glen Ferris Inn

  This Inn was built by Aaron Stockton, brother-in-law to William Tompkins, in 1839. Andrew Jackson, John Tyler, Henry Clay, and James Audubon have all been guests there. Still operating as an Inn, you can reach it on U.S. Route 60 near Gauley Bridge.

- Gauley Bridge

  Historical Society Museum

- Cathedral Falls

- Don't miss these breathtaking falls, only 3 miles from the Glen Ferris Inn.
- Ansted

  Hawk's Nest Museum
- Contentment Historical Complex,

  African-American Family Tree Museum
- Fayetteville
- Court Street Gallery, Morris Harvey House

Chapter 8

Slavery in the Kanawha Valley

> "Who would be free themselves must strike the blow....I urge you to fly to arms and smite to death the power that would bury the Government and your liberty in the same hopeless grave. This is your golden opportunity."
>
> ~Frederick Douglass

Many people are surprised to learn that slavery existed in this rugged land of wild beauty; after all, the land was settled first by Indians, then by pioneers who mostly came from Europe and other far-off lands.

But slavery did exist in the Valley, and somehow the issue of owning slaves was tangled up in the pioneers' understanding of the division of rights between the East and West. Plus, the laws were made in Richmond—and the tax laws were definitely affected by slavery.

Dick Pointer

One important slave in West Virginia history was Dick Pointer was a slave who lived in Fort Donnally in 1778, a time when Indian raids were rampant. It was common for the people inside the forts to notify other settlements of the advancement of Indian bands when they saw them. In the month of May a band of Indians were seen crossing the Ohio River near the mouth of the Great Kanawha River. Captain McKee, at Point Pleasant, sent two volunteers named John Pryor and Philip Hammond to go to Greenbrier County and let the people there know the Indians were coming.

One of Cornstalk's sisters, a friend of the white people, painted Pryor and Hammond's faces as Indians. Even though the Indians had several days' head start, the two were able to get ahead of them and warn the inhabitants of the fort.

One night the men inside the fort had not slept for nearly forty-eight hours; most of them went up to the second story and fell asleep. Only three men were left downstairs. At daybreak an Irish servant of Donally's who was downstairs with Pointer opened the kitchen door and slipped outside in order to bring in some firewood. For some reason he left the stockade gate open. Only a few steps from the house he was shot down by Indians, who had been hiding in the edge of the rye field beside the fort. Because no one knew he had gone out, no one realized the stockade gate had been left open—except the Indians who were outside.

The Indians waited until evening, then rushed the fort. Two men ran to push the stockade door shut against them. One of them was Dick Pointer, a black servant of Colonel Donally. Some reports say that Pointer stood seven feet tall. Dick Pointer and Hammond, from Point Pleasant attempted to push the door shut, but the Indians hacked at it with their tomahawks. Hammond cut down one man with his tomahawk as the Indian tried to force his way through the opening. Dick quickly loaded a musket and shot at them until he and Hammond could shut the door. The shots awakened the others, who grabbed their guns and began driving the Indians outside the stockade.

Some of the Indians did manage to get underneath the floor to try to set the building on fire, but the whites managed to life the floor and kill them. One Indian climbed a tree and shot William Black, but the bullet glanced off his forehead. Captain Jack Williams immediately shot the Indian through the head.

All in all, the whites lost four men that day.

Captain John Stuart sent a scout from Fort Savannah (which later became Lewisburg) and learned about the raid. He and about sixty-six men set out to help the people in the fort, but they were attacked by the Indians as well. They managed to get to the fort with only holes in their clothes from the bullets, but no injuries.

The Indians continued shooting until dark. An Indian then came to the fort and said they "wanted peace." They carried away their dead, except for seventeen that were left inside the stockade. Dick Pointer buried these about thirty yards from the fort the next day.

The fort was a log house, two stories high, with a kitchen one and one-half stories high. The stockade was made of split logs and was eight feet high. It stood on the east side of Rader's Creek.

Dick went before the legislature after his heroic act and was granted freedom. He was given a life lease on some land, and some people built him a cabin. He lived nearly thirty years afterward and was buried in the Lewisburg Cemetery with "war honors".

A door from the old fort was eventually taken to the State museum in the Capitol at Charleston.

The Life of a Slave

In the Kanawha Valley, the Indians welcomed escaped slaves, because the slaves could help them to learn to speak the English language. Ohio and Pennsylvania had plenty of free (white) labor, due to the existence of indentured servants; people would come to the new land as a servant for a certain number of years, then they would be free to live as they chose. The Kanawha Valley lagged behind even in the ability to own slaves; though the land was fertile with rich soil and minerals, wages here were low.

The 1800s saw that slavery in Old Virginia was becoming less profitable. The soil had been depleted by their constant planting of crops, so prices were up and down. The prices of slaves were also up and down, although the cotton gin made them somewhat more valuable. Slave owners found that they had a surplus of slaves. Ironically, the laws that had been passed for their protection did not allow them to free useless slaves, so they had to find other means of making a profit.

Typically, slaves were treated like chattel—given as property in wills, or used as bond. In towns that lined the rivers, there were very strict laws controlling the possible escape of slave men and women. The towns employed slave chaser, who would take them back across the rivers. In Charleston, patrollers kept all the blacks—even the free ones—off the streets at night.

Nat Turner's Revolt

A slave named Nat Turner was at the center of a slave rebellion that became one of the biggest events in history.

Nat Turner was born in Southampton County, Virginia in 1800. Turner was a frighteningly intelligent child; he also seemed to have knowledge of events that had happened before he was born, making people believe he was a prophet.

When Nat grew up, he became a preacher. He had three visions that he believed were from God. Nat ran away from his overseer in 1821, but then had his first vision. In it the Spirit told him to return to his master, so he did.

Three years later, he had another vision, this time seeing drops of blood on corn, hieroglyphics on the leaves in the woods, and figures portrayed in blood.

In 1828, Turner had another vision, this one was about the Serpent being loosed, and he believed that the Spirit told him to fight it. In the vision he was told to wait for a sign, then to slay his enemies.

In 1831 there was an eclipse of the sun. Turner believed this was the sign he had been promised, and he told his plan to four trusted friends. A few months later, something happened in the atmosphere to cause the sun to appear blue-green. Turner viewed this as the final sign; he and his men (now six of them) went to his master's home and killed the entire family. They went from house to house, killing white people and gathering slaves to add to their force.

After nine days of this onslaught, several of Turner's troops were captured. State and federal troops then attacked them, and one slave was killed.

In the end, Turner was one of the escapees; the men had stabled, shot, or clubbed at least 55 white people.

Nat was captured in October and imprisoned. When tried, he was sentenced to execution. Nat Turner was hanged, then skinned, on November 11.

The result of the rebellion was much more far-reaching than Nat Turner's execution; in the end the state executed 55 people, banished others, and acquitted a very few. The state even reimbursed the slaveholders for the slaves. But the real tragedy was that slaves all over the country were accused of being connected to Nat Turner's insurrection; many were tried and executed, and over 200 were lynched by white mobs. None of these slaves had anything to do with Nat Turner and his visions.

The state legislature discussed abolishing slavery, but voted to retain it.

One visitor to the Kanawha Valley was horrified to see two hundred slaves chained together and marched to the Ohio River for transport. It was very common to see such sights, as the slaves often were taken from here to Point Pleasant or to Barbourville, then Guyandotte to load onto boats. This was probably the origination of the phrase, "sold down the river."

The slave laws were severe: slaves were not considered citizens. They had no name, title, or register. They could not make a will. Slaves could be sold, mortgaged, or leased. If the slave was injured, the owner could bring a lawsuit and obtain damages from the third party.

Slaves were not allowed to practice their own religion; some came from Muslim backgrounds, and some practiced varying forms of ancestor worship. Slave owners, though, thought that African religion equaled witchcraft, so they banned it. They wanted to Christianize their slaves in order to make them more passive. They taught the slaves the Bible in a selective way, so that the New Testament messages about individual freedom and responsibility could not be passed on.

Slaves could not possess arms, and by law could not be allowed to read or write. They had no civil rights whatsoever. But the growing population of free blacks also encountered some rather draconian laws; for example, once they were set free, they must leave the state which they lived in after no more than twelve months—often leaving behind a spouse or children, if they had not been freed. Many of those slaves ended up settling here, in the Kanawha Valley.

It was common for owners to lease the slaves out to the iron industry to produce income. As the prices for tobacco declined in Eastern Virginia, large numbers of slaves were sent here to work in the salt mines; the number of slaves in the Kanawha Valley area tripled around 1810 to 1820. They were worked on a schedule of four hours on, four hours off around the clock. That way, an owner could get a lot more hours out of them during a 24-hour day. Even the small children were put to work on this schedule. Slaves were also the first to be made to cut trees for the timber industry, then later they were put to work mining coal.

Old records of slaves, found in the West Virginia Archives, show that the Jenkins family owned the largest number of slaves. The slaves were only listed as a head count, not by name. An 1850 census shows that there were 12,000 whites in the area, compared with 3,000 blacks.

Since the census count only showed the white and black populations, we wonder how the Indians were counted. The census doesn't tell us, but we do know that Indians were forced to go to black schools.

In 1863, West Virginia was a slave state, but they had no clear agreement about abolition.

In May of 1863, the U.S. War department established a "bureau of Colored Troops" to help recruit African-American soldiers for the Union Army. About 175 regiments were formed made up of over 178,000 free blacks. The 45th U.S. Colored Infantry of West Virginia was made up of black men from Virginia, West Virginia, and Pennsylvania. Most of the men were free, either having been freed or having escaped from their owners. The 45th had over 220 soldiers, but most of their medals are still unclaimed, largely due to the fact that good records were not kept of the black population and since many people were illiterate there are lots of spelling discrepancies.

Although black soldiers were instrumental in the war, discrimination was widely practiced. Soldiers were to receive $10.00 per month and a clothing allowance of $3.50 according to the Militia Act; some regiments refused any money at all until 1864 when Congress granted equal pay for all black soldiers.

Booker T. Washington

One of the best-known African-Americans from the Charleston area was Booker T. Washington. Born in Hale's Ford, Va. in 1856 to a mother who was a mulatto plantation slave; his father was a white man. His mother learned that she was free in the spring of 1865 but was still on the Franklin county, Virginia farm trying to decide what she should do, when a message came to her from West Virginia that her husband, Booker's stepfather, was working at the salt furnaces of the Kanawha Salines in West Virginia. He sent Jane money to buy a wagon, and she and her three children set out to join him.

The children walked most of the 200 miles to the Kanawha River. Jane's health prevented her from walking, so she rode in the wagon. They eventually found their father in a cabin in Malden. They moved in and tried to settle into a life there. Booker found the area to be crowded, smelly, and filthy; he never got over his distaste for the filth and immorality of town living.

The Kanawha salt industry had reached a great decline by the time Booker's family arrived in Malden. It isn't clear whether the family knew this prior to coming to Malden or not. His stepfather, Washington Ferguson, worked at John P. Hale's Snow Hill Furnace packing salt into barrels for shipment.

Booker soon learned that his stepfather had sent for him and his brother to come to Malden in order to make them assist him in packing the salt. The crystals had to be shoveled into barrels then pounded until the barrel reached the right weight. The workday was long, beginning at 4 a.m. and continuing until dark. Their stepfather took all their pay for himself, never giving the boys a dime for their trouble.

None of the slaves back in Booker's birth place, Hale's Ford, could read; nor could the blacks in Malden. But Booker met a man from Ohio who could read the newspaper, and he discovered his intense desire to learn to read. He listened to the man read aloud every day. His mother bought him a spelling book and he was quickly on his way.

A school opened at Tinkersville for the black children, but Booker's stepfather would not allow him to attend. It isn't known whether he was too poor to let his son remain at home without working to pay for his keep, or whether children were that valuable in the salt furnaces. Yet Booker kept his intense desire for learning. Finally, a deal was struck; Ferguson allowed Booker to go to school if he would go to the salt furnace to work from 4 a.m. to 9 a.m., then return to the furnace after school for two hours. After a few years of this schedule, the biggest move that Washington had made yet occurred: he left the family home with its bad smells and street brawls and the difficult life Wash Ferguson put him through, and he became the houseboy to General Lewis Ruffner and his wife, Viola.

Lewis Ruffner had been the first white child born in Charleston in 17899; his family was a leading family of the "better class". Lewis owned twenty-six slaves in 1860, and leased others to work in his numerous businesses: furnaces, mines, and farms.

Viola Ruffner had a reputation as an exacting mistress, and Booker soon tired of her badgering and ran away. He managed to get passage on a steamboat as a cabin boy, but the captain quickly discovered that he didn't know anything about the job. He wanted to toss Booker off the boat, but Booker persuaded him to let him hitch a ride back to Malden. He returned to Mrs. Ruffner—in fact, she said that he left numerous times, but he always came back. Mrs. Ruffner encouraged him to attend school, taught him to read, and helped him to begin his own library. When she grew too much produce for her family to eat, she encouraged Booker to go out and sell it. He not only did so, he made a handsome profit, and always brought back every penny of income to give to her.

Booker was able to enter the Hampton Institute in Virginia to get an education, where a friend of the principal paid his tuition. He worked as a janitor at the school to pay for his room and board. After gaining an education, he returned to Malden for a short time and taught school for African American children. Later he attended Wayland Seminary, then was appointed as an instructor at Hampton Institute. He also was chosen to organize a school for African Americans at Tuskegee, AL. the Tuskegee University became a leading educational institution in America. Booker used the University to push the African American population to acquire skills that would help them to become reliable, responsible citizens. He founded the National Negro Business League to further black advancement.

A discussion about Booker T. Washington wouldn't be complete without talking about his speeches. He spoke in 1895 in Atlanta, Ga. Encouraging blacks to gain economic equality before they fought for social equality, which hardly gained a good position among African-American leaders (although the whites liked it). Booker T. Washington received honorary degrees from Dartmouth and Harvard Universities.

Washington wrote several books, including a top non-fiction work called *Up From Slavery*. He died on November 14, 1915 at Tuskegee.

If you go there...

Malden is on the Midland Trail and has dedicated the downtown area to history. At the African Baptist Zion Church, circa 1872, you will find the spirit of the legacy of Booker T. Washington. This was the first black Baptist Church in Western Virginia; the African-American families who started it were respected workers in the salt mines. Directly behind the church are prototype living quarters, a schoolhouse, and artifacts from Booker's era. The cabin was rebuilt to match a photograph of Booker T. Washington's home; for tours, call 304-925-9499.Across the street is the foundation of his sister's home, now a beautiful park.

While in Malden, don't forget to visit Norton house, the oldest frame house in Malden. Originally built by Moses Norton and James G. Norton, father-son businessmen, Norton House was renovated in 1994 by Cabin Creek Quilts.

The Hale House, home of Dr. John P. Hale, was Charleston's elegant railroad hotel.

The 1840 Kanawha Salines Presbyterian Church was organized in 1819 by the Ruffner family. Dr. Henry Ruffner was President of Washington College, later named Washington and Lee College. He was known for a controversial paper that he wrote advocating abolition of slavery in America. While you're visiting the church, be sure to observe the offering; poles with bags on the ends are used to collect them, as was done 175 years ago.

Take exit 96 off I77/64. Follow the Midland Trail east 1 mile to the Malden exit.

The education of Negroes was perhaps more forward-thinking in Kanawha County and other counties located along the C&O railroad than in other areas. Early settlements from the influx into the salt works, and later the coal mines, led to many so-called Negro schools in the area. A 1920 Charleston census showed the area's population to be 84 percent white. The rest of the population was divided evenly between Negro and foreign-born residents, at eight percent each. By 1930, the black population in the state was nearly 20,000.

Coal Mining

When the first carload of coal was shipped on the Norfolk and Western Railway in 1883, it opened up southwestern West Virginia to a new world of business. Population increased, new towns originated, and the region quickly became industrial. European immigrants rushed to West Virginia seeking good salaries and cheap housing. At the same time many African Americans came from the southern states.

The workers soon found out that the company controlled everything. They had to lease their tools from the company and rent their homes from them. The company then deducted the costs from their wages. They paid them in scrip instead of money. This scrip had to be used at the company store. Even when wages were increased the company just raised the prices at the company store.

Miners were paid based upon the tons of coal they mined. The company set a certain amount per car, but the cars held more than they were paid for. They also docked their wages for slate and rock mixed with the coal. Since it was at the company's discretion, miners frequently were docked for more than necessary.

Safety in the mines soon became a major problem. West Virginia was the site of many deadly coal mining accidents. In fact, from 1890 to 1912, West Virginia had the dubious distinction of owning the highest coal mine death rate in the entire country.

Because of the safety concerns, low wages, and poor economic conditions, workers in many industries started unions. Strikes stopped production, and attempts to create a union failed as late as 1897. They finally established a union in 1902. The Kanawha County Coal Operators hired private detectives to harass union organizers which discouraged them from working in southern West Virginia. The union subsequently lost control of this mine.

After the miners lost their union, they joined the Paint Creek strikers and demanded fair wages and the right to a union among other things.

Operators brought in guards to evict miners and their families from company houses. Their job was to make the lives as uncomfortable as possible in order to break the strike.

National labor leaders began helping the strikers. They sent speechmakers, weapons and ammunition. The governor imposed martial law and sent troops three different times.

When the violence began, one of the armored trains rolled through a ten colony and killed a striker. The miners attacked an encampment and sixteen people were killed.

When West Virginians swore Henry D. Hatfield in as governor, he set the terms for settlement of the strike. He honed in on the demands of the striking miners and ordered them to accept his terms. The only two demands that they didn't agree upon were the right to organize and the removal of mine guards. They finally settled the strike by removing the detectives and mine guards.

After the strikes the coalfields were peaceful until the US entered World War I. When the war ended and the recession began, the companies tried to reduce wages to pre-war levels. This caused the workers to strike again. Non-union mines were dynamited, miners' tent colonies were attacked, and many people were killed. The coal operators paid the sheriff (Chafin) to keep the union organizers out. They paid for deputies to help him.

In late 1919 the operators lowered wages yet again. The Coal Commission gave a wage increase to union miners but excluded the southwestern West Virginia miners. Families of miners who joined the union were evicted from company-owned houses. The chief of police, Sid Hatfield, encouraged the people to acquire weapons. When detectives attempted to arrest Hatfield, seven people were killed. In late summer, Sid Hatfield, was killed while walking to trial for a shooting at a coal camp.

Hatfield became a hero to many miners. They began assembling in Charleston to protest the killing. The governor requested federal troops. President Harding sent World War I hero Henry Bandholtz to assess the situation. He and the governor met with two leaders and told them that they needed to be turned back or be charged with treason. Some of the miners did turn aback at that time, but many others marched on. Chafin's forces battled with them and some were killed.

Next, President Harding sent federal troops from Kentucky under the leadership of Billy Mitchell. When the first federal troops arrived, most of the miners surrender or returned home. The ones that surrendered were placed on trains and sent homes. The leaders were to be held accountable for the miners' actions. Twenty-four indictments for treason against the state were handed down, along with some for murder. One of the treason trials was held in the Jefferson County Courthouse in Charles Town which is where John Brown had been convicted of treason in 1859. The man was Bill Blizzard whom the authorities considered to be the miners' "general." All charges against Blizzard were dropped as well as most of the other charges against miners.

The defeat of the miners ended the union's efforts to organize until 1933 when the National Industrial Recovery Act protected the right to belong to a union and allowed then to quickly organize in the southern coalfields. The United Mine Workers of America now continues in its mission to ensure that miners have, in addition to the right to organize, rights to free speech, assembly, and unions that can oversee the companies to be sure workers aren't cheated, among others. The UMWA has been instrumental in ensuring health and safety for workers; in 1969 they encouraged Congress to enact the Federal Coal Mine Health and Safety Act, which was the first time that Congress mandated the eradication of a disease that man created (Black Lung).

Chapter 9

Transportation in the Kanawha Valley

Railways

The Mountain State has always been known for its physical barriers to travel and for the ways that its inhabitants try to overcome them. Settlements were created on the navigable rivers and near natural breaks in the mountains in order to make travel as easy as possible. The heavily forested mountains offered a wealth of lumber, rich deposits of coal, natural gas and oil; these reserves were largely inaccessible until the coming of the rails. Mountain roads were crude and often rendered impassable due to weather; much of West Virginia remained separate from the rest of the world even after most of the country had well-established transportation. Business men in the 1800s quickly realized that if industry were to prosper, railroads had to be built.

The B&O is the oldest railroad in the U.S., and more than 210 of its 379 miles lie in West Virginia. It was constructed by Baltimore and the state of Maryland in hopes that it would serve as a link to the agricultural

Midwest, to commerce offered by the Ohio River and to increase the city's industrial standing.

The Baltimore and Ohio was completed as far as Wheeling on Christmas Eve, 1852. The line passed through Harpers Ferry and Grafton. Eventually Grafton became a dual station that also served the Northwestern Virginia Railroad. It would later connect with Parkersburg.

Many of the West Virginia battles and skirmishes during the Civil were the result of the struggle to control the region's railroads. There was little true damage; soldiers wished to control the delivery of supplies, not destroy the lines. The period after the war was the era of the railway for West Virginia.

Construction in the mountains proved to be a challenge, to say the least. The Chesapeake and Ohio Line, which connected Richmond, Virginia, and Huntington, faced enormous barriers. Tunnels had to be blasted and drilled through the mountains giving birth not only to a rail line, but to legends as well. One legend concerns the Big Bend Tunnels near Hinton and John Henry, the "Steel Drivin' Man" who was immortalized in song. In fact, a statue near the site of that epic contest commemorates the story of John Henry's competition with a steam drill. The company had completed much of the work around the Charleston area prior to the Civil War, but the war drew construction nearly to a standstill.

One of the first trunk lines built in West Virginia after the Civil War, the Chesapeake and Ohio Railway was begun in 1868; the rails were connected at Hawks Nest on January 29, 1873. The C&O line followed the pathways created by Native Americans as well as stagecoach routes. It entered the state east of White Sulphur Springs in Greenbrier County and traveled along the New River, then followed the Kanawha River for several miles and cut across to Huntington and the Ohio River. Collis P. Huntington later extended the line to Louisville, New Orleans and westward, thus further opening trade to the South, the West and broadening the prominence of rural West Virginia. Local residents say that Collis Huntington established the new city after being arrested in nearby Guyandotte for riding his horse on the sidewalk.

The completion of the line in 1873 meant the opening of the Kanawha River Valley to industrialization. The railroad also made possible the intensive mining operations that fueled the state's economy. In 1892, the Norfolk and Western Railroad opened its Ohio Extension which was built expressly for the purpose of opening up the rich Pocahontas coal field in southwestern West Virginia. Many of West Virginia's most renowned and colorful historical figures are associated with the rail industry. Collis P. Huntington, H. H. Rogers, Henry Gassaway Davis and Stephen Benton Elkins all had a hand in expanding the railway system; therefore they also had a hand in bringing prosperity and development to West Virginia.

The Blue Creek train, of the Kanawha and West Virginia Railroad Line, began running in 1907 from Charleston to Blakely, a coal town. Its track was extended to Hitop, a total of 34.4 miles, during World War I.

The train was used to haul timber as well as coal from the oil field—but, like many others in the 20th century, it soon became a passenger train. It was the main source of news for many, even blowing its whistle in a pattern to announce the winners and losers of local elections.

The train also was used as an ambulance and a hearse, when the occasion called for it. It was the only reliable source of transportation, especially in the winter; so students were given tickets to ride the train by the school board. They probably got as much education in the ways of life on the train as they did about more practical matters inside the classroom. Sometimes the students skipped school and rode the trail on into Charleston for the day.

In the 1930s, all the railroad lines were busy adding tunnels, track, rebuilding bridges and roadbeds, and upgrading rail weights. That's because so much money had been made hauling bituminous coal. Every the Great Depression didn't hamper the use of coal, which everyone had to have.

This meant that the C&O was prepared to carry the incredible amount of men and materials during the war. The war also caused a need for greater amounts of coal, and C&O was ready to help provide that.

After numerous mergers of more modern railroads, C&O has come out as CSX, one of only four major railroad systems in the country.

If you go there...

The Charleston Capitol Market is a location you won't want to miss on your visit. The Capitol Market is open year-round in an airy revamped train depot that's reminiscent of its roots when it was an open air market. The ambience will transport to days gone by; enjoy lunch or shop for local West Virginia foods, vegetables, books, and wines.

C&O DEPOT, 4th Ave St. Albans

This restored depot, constructed around 1906, fronts one of St. Albans' original brick streets. Tall windows, high ceilings and other touches make this one of the more architecturally detailed depots in the state.

The depot was turned over to the City of St. Albans in the late 1980s and was leased by the St. Albans Women's Club, then by the present group, Friends of the Depot. The group worked to acquire grants, volunteer labor, and materials to restore the Depot to its original appearance.

A Freight Depot once stood adjacent to the Train Depot. In its place is now a structure that was built in 1998 by the St. Albans Historical Society. The Depot was listed on the National Register of Historic Places in 1998.

The Depot Museum is filled with Railroad photos and artifacts to delight every train enthusiast. It is open by appointment.

Open Houses are conducted for special functions; The Depot is available for rent for receptions, Reunions, showers and other events. Phone 727-3084.

New River Train Trips

The Collis P. Huntington Railroad Historical Society, Amtrak, and CSX cooperate to provide four separate one-day round trip excursions each year in October. The non-profit CPH society has operated these trips nearly every year for the past forty years.

The trip originates in Huntington West Virginia, stops in Albans to receive passengers from Charleston, and stops in Montgomery before arriving in Hinton. The layover lasts approximately three hours so that passengers can visit a street fair featuring arts, crafts, food, and entertainment.

Chapter 10

Famous People

One person who appreciated Charleston in all its beauty was John F. Kennedy, who established his headquarters in the Kanawha Hotel in 1960. After winning the state primary, Kennedy praised the people of West Virginia, claiming that they had made his nomination for president possible.

The hotel was built in 1903 and was open until 1965, then reopened as an office space until the 1990s. It was purchased for Job Corps in 1996.

Mother Jones

> "There is no peace in West Virginia, because there is no justice in West Virginia."
>
> —Mother Jones

The American industrial revolution brought on many changes, not all of them positive. Industry widely practiced the exploitation of immigrant workers, imposed poor working conditions, and created overcrowded cities. The 1880s saw child labor suffering, 17-hour work days, mass unemployment, and the birth of one of America's greatest leaders—Mother Jones. If there was anyone who helped West Virginians achieve a higher standard of living, it was Mother Jones. She was instrumental in fighting to give all citizens equal civil rights.

Mother Jones was born in 1830 in Cork, Ireland. Her name was Mary Harris. As a child in Ireland, she saw British soldiers march through the streets with the heads of Irishmen stuck on their Bayonets. Her grandfather had been hanged for being a freedom fighter; her father had to flee to America with his family in 1835. She spent most of her life as a teacher and dressmaker. She eventually married and moved to Memphis, Tennessee. In 1867, yellow fever took her husband and all four of her children. After this tragedy, Mary Harris Jones helped nurse other sufferers until the epidemic was over. When the disease seemed to have gotten under control, she moved to Chicago to work as a dressmaker.

But tragedy struck again. This time the Great Chicago Fire of 1871 claimed her business establishment, which was also her home, and everything she owned. After the Chicago fire, Mother Jones joined the Knights of Labor, an organization formed after the Civil War to fight against industrial slavery. Her father and husband had been hard working laborers, so her decision to take an active part in the efforts of the working class was a natural one. Mother Jones traveled on foot between the coal camps from West Virginia to Colorado, and to mills and factories from Illinois to Georgia fighting for the freedom of the working class. In West Virginia, she was the first walking delegate for the United Mine Workers of America, pushing miners to risk their lives to form a union.

Mother Jones often involved the wives and children of miners to dramatize a situation. On September 21, 1912, she led a march of miners' children through the streets of Charleston. Mother Jones was jailed two times for leading union strikes in West Virginia; once in 1902 at age 71, and again in 1913 at 82. This second arrest took place in Charleston just after she debarked from a Kanawha & Michigan passenger train in the company of a committee of miners from Smithers (30 miles east). She had been making her headquarters in Charleston at the Fleetwood Hotel. The police waited for her arrival, as they felt she was coming here to address the strike trouble in the Kanawha Valley.

The policemen accosted the party and showed Mother Jones a warrant, informing her that she was under arrest. The other members of the party were permitted to go on their way.

Mrs. Jones did not resist in any way; she was taken to the Hotel Ruffner by taxi with the officers. The group waited at the hotel until nearly time for the arrival of C. & O. train No. 8, which happened to be running a few minutes late that day. She was then escorted to the depot on the South Side depot along with a man named Paul Paulson. Paulson was arrested about the same time as Mother Jones, also in connection with the strike trouble.

Mother Jones and Mr. Paulson rode on train No. 8 to Pratt, where they were handed over to the military authorities. They were held at the station house at Pratt with numerous other strikers who had also been arrested for rioting.

The court convicted Mother Jones of conspiring to commit murder; she was sentenced to 20 years in prison. Her sentence created such a ruckus, though, that the Senate ordered a committee to investigate the conditions in the West Virginia coalfields.

The newly elected governor quickly set Mother Jones free.

Mother Jones took up her cause yet again in 1914, when 20 miners and their families were killed in the "Machine-gun massacre" in Ludlow, Colorado. Mother Jones traveled the country telling the story to all who would hear it. She believed, "In spite of oppressors, in spite of false leaders, in spite of labor's own lack of understanding of its needs, the cause of the working class continues onward. Slowly his standard of living rises to include some of the good and beautiful things of the world ... Slowly those who create the wealth of the world are permitted to share it. The future is in labor's strong hands."

She died seven months after her 100th birthday, still active in striving to achieve a positive outcome of the labor movement. Jones is buried in the United Mine Workers Cemetery in Mount Olive, Illinois, near the victims of the 1898 riot. More than 30,000 people attended her funeral.

On January 28, 1993, Mother Jones was inducted into the Labor Hall of Fame in Washington, D.C. A plaque in her honor states: "For countless workers she was both goad and inspiration... Her flaming rhetoric and fearless campaigning helped swell the ranks of the United Mine Workers who called her the Miner's Angel."

Doors from "Mother Jones Prison" in Pratt were used in the rebuilt Booker T. Washington cabin. Her "prison" was actually a boarding house, where she lived in 1913 after a Military court convicted her of murder for her role in the Paint Creek/Cabin Creek Mine War.

Cabin Creek Quilts has kept the secret trap door which Mother Jones was said to have used to pass letters to the press from inside a closet. It was originally positioned under the boarding house staircase. Her actions created international outrage over the mine wars.

Hubert Humphrey

Hubert Humphrey was known for his big heart, but few knew that it was more tender than the heart found among most men of power. When one night in West Virginia he lost the critical presidential primary to John Kennedy, his tender heart was like a gaping wound for a few minutes. But he quickly recuperated; it was said that he retreated to his room at the old Ruffner Hotel and calmly made himself a sandwich.

James Audubon

James Audubon, of Haitian descent, came to America in 1803 at the age of 18. He started out living in Pennsylvania, but spent his life traveling up and down the Ohio and Kanawha Rivers, among other areas, looking for birds that he could paint and describe. When in Charleston, Audubon stayed at the Holly Grove Mansion (located in the State Capitol Complex).

Audubon conducted some of the first known bird-banding in the United States, trying to see if the birds returned to the same nesting sites every year.

Audubon's life-size wildlife prints would rival those of any 20th or 21st century bird artist. His name is now synonymous with birding conservation. Audubon actually was not connected to the organization that bears his name; the name was chosen in his honor.

Simon Kenton

Simon Kenton, along with two companions whose names we do not know, built a cabin at the mouth of the Elk River in 1771. This made Kenton and his friends the first Englishmen to call present-day Kanawha County their home. Soon after, a band of Indians discovered these intruders on their hunting grounds and attacked them, killing one of the men in the attack. After escaping the attack, Simon Kenton and his remaining friend decided to leave the county for good.

Chapter 11

Charleston Today

Today Charleston continues to bustle with activity, whether it be cultural, political, or social in nature. The wide river sparkles as coal barges regularly traverse up and down its winding curves. Charleston's rolling hills are close enough for you to explore if you want to, yet you can still enjoy the ambience of a capital city.

At every time of the year, Charleston has delightful pleasures to offer. Downtown activities never cease. Foot tours through the Capitol Complex or the magnificent old neighborhoods can be taken at nearly any time.

If you tire of the beauty, consider turning to the SouthRidge Shopping Center. Or try out some of the many boutiques located in the Renaissance Village. Don't forget to try one of the many restaurants, which range from family-style comfort to fine dining.

Charleston's activities, recreation, and attractions make it a prime location for a quick getaway, a leisurely vacation, or even a new place to call home. On the next pages, I'll try to outline some of the attractions and activities there are to enjoy in Charleston. This list is by no means complete; it could have gone on and on. There has to be a stopping point somewhere, so I have called it. I hope you will explore at least some of these options and will find Charleston to be at once peaceful, yet sophisticated. Enjoy!

South Charleston

South Charleston was formed in 1916, with the establishment of several chemical companies there. South Charleston was once known as the chemical capitol of the world; the Kanawha Valley Chemical Industry was instrumental in building the area, beginning with the Rollins chemical Company in 1913 and continuing to expand into the present. The Union Carbide Water Tower was constructed in 1958. Union Carbide, a subsidiary of Dow Chemical Company has two operations there.

Nearby are the historically significant office buildings on MacCorkle Avenue, which is surrounded by the various laboratories, businesses, and other organizations that were built to serve the industry's employees. The South Charleston site manufactures about 400 million pounds of chemicals and plastics every year.

Despite the name, South Charleston doesn't really lie south of the city of Charleston; remember, you're in the Mountain State and between mountains and rivers, things can be slightly askew. South Charleston lies northwest of the city of Charleston. At any rate, it is a diverse area that blends the old and new seamlessly together. The area considers itself a separate area from main Charleston; it offers city amenities, yet small-town charm. South Charleston is within a short drive of all the attractions of West Virginia, yet also offers its own share of antiques, unique shopping, and cultural activities.

If you go there...

Little Creek Park

This park has West Virginia's only lighted Soap Box Derby Track. The track hosts races and events from spring through fall of every year. There are also eleven picnic shelters available for rental. All are equipped with electricity, grills and fireplaces. Restrooms and recreational equipment are available. The park is open from March 1 through October 31, seven days a week from 8:30 a.m. to 10:30 p.m. it is located off of Spring Hill Avenue on the west side of South Charleston.

The South Charleston Memorial Ice Arena has an arcade, a heated seating area, and an official size rink. The rink is used for hockey, figure skating, and public skating. The bleachers seat 500 people. Skating lessons are available for all ages. A pro-shop can provide you with all the latest in skates and wearing apparel. Party rooms are available for rent, with an arcade and concessions on premises. Open to the public.

One of the largest recreational facilities in the area is the South Charleston Community Center; it boasts an indoor pool, racquetball, basketball, tanning beds, and a health club. The Center's gym seats 1500 and hosts a variety of activities. Open daily; the two racquetball courts can be rented by the hour. for reservations or more information call (304) 744-4815.

Attractions

Architectural Landmarks

405 Capitol Street

Formerly the Daniel Boone Hotel, one of Charleston's most lavish hotels, this 1929 landmark was built by a progressive group of Charleston citizens at a cost of more than $1.2 million. It was named for Daniel Boone, frontiersman, who spent several years as a resident of Kanawha County. This hotel has been the temporary home to numerous celebrities: John F. Kennedy, Bob Hope, Tyrone Power, and Elvis Presley. The exterior has been maintained as an historical structure, while the interior has been revamped as office space; it is often cited for its incredible 10-story atrium. Located at 405 Capitol Street.

Brawley Walkway and Slack Plaza

This walkway connects Capitol Street to Court Street, and serves as a link between the renovated downtown and Charleston Town Center mall. The walkway was named for Harry Brawley, who lived from 1910-1992, was a historian who worked in the area as a high school and college teacher, radio and TV personality, and Charleston councilman. Brawley is said to have done more for the city's history than any other individual. He knew the history of every building and family in Charleston, but more importantly he chronicled these stories for publication in magazines.

Between Summers and Laidley Street, the walkway broadens out to become Slack Plaza and Transportation Mall. This favorite gathering place was named in honor of former Congressman John M. Slack. Slack attended public schools in Charleston, graduated from VMI, and served on the Kanawha County Court and as the Kanawha County assessor.

Burning Springs Monument

This monument was built to commemorate the first drilled well in America and the first industrial use of natural gas at Burning Springs.

The monument is located on US Route 60 East of Charleston, near the Capitol Complex.

C & O Railroad Depot

This Beaux Arts-style brick building with terra cotta trim provided the state capital with a grand point of interest in earlier days. Originally constructed in 1905, it was completely refurbished inside and out in 1987 in order to restore it to its original style. AT that time a companion structure in the same style was erected beside it. The old depot houses a restaurant on the main level with office space on the upper level. It also still houses the local depot for AMTRAK.

Located at 350 MacCorkle Ave, SE.

Cabriole/BB&T Square

The sculpture Cabriole is located at the entrance to the BB&T building. Cabriole is made from cast bronze and depicts three male dancers who are engaged in a dance step known as the "cabriole" (a type of leap into the air). The sculpture was dedicated in 1981. It is about 8 feet high and 14 feet wide; each figure weighs about 600 pounds. The sculptor, Jimilu Mason of Arlington, VA., referred to the work as her "grandest project ever." It is said that she took three years to complete it. The sculpture can be seen at the intersection of Summers and Lee Street.

City Hall

Charleston's city hall building was designed in 1922 by H. Rus Warne, architect. It features fluted columns rising for the length of two stories, lending classical dignity to the front elevation of Charleston's handsome seat of government. City Hall is located at the intersection of Court and Virginia Streets.

Commerce Square

Originally a domed Beaux Arts-style building constructed over the period from 1901 to 1903, this was the site of the Old Statehouse Annex. It was home to the West Virginia Supreme Court and State Archives. It is now the site of a glass and metal tower and contains the Huntington Banks West Virginia building. The building is located in the 800 Block of Lee Street.

Coyle & Richardson Building

This 3-story brick structure was built in the 1890s and was the site of the dry goods company called Coyle and Richardson. Notice the extremely detailed brick-work and ornate decoration. The building stands at the corner of Lee and Dickinson Streets.

First Presbyterian Church

This church was established in 1819; the current building was designed by Weaver, Werner, and Atkins, architects in 1915. One of the great architectural land-marks of West Virginia, the church displays an Imperial Roman exterior and a breathtaking Byzantine interior, including a 52-foot diameter dome and a spectacular traditional pipe organ. The Church is located one block off Kanawha Boulevard at the corner of Virginia Street and Leon Sullivan Way; 16 Leon Sullivan Way. The church building is open every day from 8 a.m. to 4 p.m.

Kanawha Presbyterian Church

This church was designed by Edwin Anderson, architect. It was built over a period of years from 1873 to 1885. It is Charleston's oldest extant house of worship, and stands as a significant example of High Victorian

Gothic architecture. Its interior is aglow with color from Tiffany glass windows.

You can visit the church at 1009 Virginia Street, East.

Kanawha Valley Building

This 20-story high-rise is richly appointed with gray and orange terra cotta trim. One of Charleston's tallest structures, it overlooks Davis Park and is surrounded by other business structures like AT&T, BB&T, and the Diamond building. It served as headquarters of the Kanawha Valley Bank and occupies the site of the old West Virginia Capitol Building which burned in 1921. The building was constructed circa 1929. 300 Capitol Street. Located on the corner of Capitol and Lee and Dickinson Streets.

Masonic Building

H. Rus Warne, architect designed this pinnacled building in 1915. Its Gothic, pointed arches and window tracery are terra cotta details that won't be found in many cities, and certainly are not duplicated even in today's modern buildings. 107 Hale Street.

One Bridge Place

This is a five-story structure that is used as an office rental space. Originally the location of the first wholesale grocery distribution firm of Lewis, Hubbard, & Company, the warehouse was burned to the ground in 1887. In 1898 the warehouse was rebuilt; since then the building has been headquarters to numerous businesses. It has been restored to its 1898 beauty, including exposing all columns, beams, and interior brick walls as well as installing period lighting and using special cleaning and restoration techniques.

Be sure to take note of the environmental mural which is located on the side of the building facing the Southside Bridge. This mural, incorporating the actual windows in the building, was conceived and painted by Bart Davies, a Fine Arts graduate of Penn State. It took two years to complete.

Virginia and Hale Streets (at the foot of the Southside Bridge).

Payne Building

It is thought that construction of the Payne House probably occurred in the 1930s. Its structures offers one of the most beautiful buildings in Charleston; marble, terra cotta, mosaic tiles and unusual ornamentation blend together to offer one of the most architecturally interesting structures in West Virginia. 819 Lee Street.

Pumpkin House

Over 3000 jack o'lanterns are each carved with a unique pattern every October; they are lit from dawn til dusk throughout the month. The home that is now known as the Pumpkin House was once owned by Joseph Miller, who was the first commissioner of the Internal Revenue Service. It was built in 1891. It is said that President Grover Cleveland once paid a visit here. Located in Kenova at 748 Beech St.

Ramsdell House

Listed on the National Register of Historic Places, this brick home was built about 1857. It was the first brick house in Ceredo and was believed to be part of the Underground Railroad.Ramsdell House hosts school tours and special events. Located at 1108 B Street, Ceredo; take exit 1 off I-64, follow Route 60 to Ceredo, and turn left onto B street.

Huntington's Rose Garden

Since 1934, West Virginia's nationally recognized municipal rose garden containing over 2,000 bushes and noted for its All-America Rose Selections. Roses of all types and colors are featured here; they have names like "St. Patrick" and Queen Elisabeth." It is an accredited testing garden and is often the site of weddings and receptions as well as other special events.

Located in Ritter Park off McCoy Road (8th Street Hill). To get there, take I-64 Exit 8 or 11. For more information, phone (304) 696-5954 or visit http://www.ghprd.org/

Sacred Heart Co-Cathedral

Great arches, expansive walls, and a monumental tower are features of the church whose cornerstone was laid by Bishop Donahue of Wheeling in late July, 1895. Romanesque-style sconces with bronze finish as well as translucent glass were installed in 1950; also around that time the red Verona and Belgian Rouge marble was placed around the sanctuary walls. The walls of the nave and vestibule feature Fleuri Travernelle marble.

The church's bell tower rises more than 120 feet above you if you're standing on Leon Sullivan Way. The large bell weighs 2,060 pounds; the middle one 1500 pounds; and the smallest, 700 pounds. The bells are rung three times a day, as they have been since June of 1901. Also above the Cathedral entrance on Leon Sullivan Way you will see a statue, cast in bronze, of the Sacred Heart, which has stood there since 1897. Located at Leon Sullivan Way and Virginia Street.

Scott Building

This structure was built in 1891 for brothers W.D. and G.W. Scott; after 1914 it was known as the Scott Brothers Drug Store & Soda Fountain, an early Charleston cornerstone. The Queen Anne-Renaissance-style features pressed brick and Victorian turrets. If you look next door, you will see the First Empire Federal Savings and Loan Association building. This was once the site of the famed Burlew Opera House, a glittering 1,500 seat theatre. Located at the corner of Fife and Capitol Streets.

Security Building

Originally the Kanawha National Bank, the building was constructed by John S. Atkins, architect. Its white glazed tiles are intricately detailed and unique to the area. Located on the N.E. corner of Capitol and Virginia Streets.

Shrewsbury Street

This street features sites and buildings that figure prominently into West Virginia's African-American history. Among these are the Sam Starks House, located at 413 Shrewsbury St. Sam Starks was a Charleston native who lived from 1866 to 1908 and was a nationally known African-American leader. He achieved many levels of acclaim, including being appointed as the first black state librarian in the U.S. Shrewsbury Street runs between the 1000 block of Washington Street and Lewis Street.

St. George Orthodox Church

This church actually formed its roots in 1892 when a group of immigrants rented a building for worship at 213 Kanawha Street, Charleston. In 1932 the current building was constructed. Its "onion" domes represent candle flames. They rise gracefully above the polychrome brick facade of the building. Of special beauty is the church's iconostasis which serves to separate the chancel from the nave. Located at Lee and Court Streets.

St. John's Episcopal Church

The original St. John's Episcopal Church was a brick building situated on the northwest corner of Virginia and McFarland Streets; it was designed by Isaac Pursell and built and consecrated in 1839. Used by the Union army during the Civil War, the building was later repaired and refurbished; however, the congregation decided to move to the current structure in 1888. This building exhibits the best elements of both Gothic and Romanesque design; a heavy base is topped by high-pitched roofs and an enormous tower. The parish house was built in 1928. Both are on the National Register of Historic Places. Located at 1105 Quarrier Street.

St. Mark's Episcopal

This church got its Kanawha Valley beginnings in 1825, when Morris Hudson built a small brick church behind his house on the old Kanawha Turnpike. The church at that time was called Bangor Parish, after Hudson's home church in Pennsylvania. This was the Episcopal place of worship until it was burned. The new structure was built in 1847 after fire destroyed the original church. Several items from the old church, like the lecturn and a Bible were brought from the Bangor parish sanctuary; the bell in the old tower is also from the original church. It was occupied by federal troops during the Civil War and almost destroyed, as they tore up the grounds and even removed the floors. Later restored, it was nearly 50 years before the federal government paid for damages. Located on "B" Street near 4th Avenue in St. Albans. Church offices are open from 8:30 a.m. to 2 p.m. daily.

St. Marks Methodist Church

This church was built in 1912. Featuring a dome tiled in green and a Corinthian portico, St. Marks seems to be patterned after ancient Rome's great Pantheon. The stately broad columns are carefully carved. 900

Washington St., East. Take I-64E to the Leon Sullivan Way/Capital Street exit (Exit 100). Turn right at the first light onto Washington Street. Turn right onto Dickinson street to enter the parking lot which is located behind the church.

Statue of St. Francis of Assisi

This statue stands in the courtyard of St. Francis Hospital and is the work of William D. Hopen, a West Virginia artist from Sutton, WV. Other works of Mr. Hopen include the statue of Booker T. Washington on the State Capitol grounds and "Mother With Children" located at the Mother's Day Shrine in Grafton, West Virginia. View the statue at 333 Laidley Street.

Terminal Building

Constructed in 1910, this eight-story office building was originally the National City Bank building. Fine cream-colored terra cotta trim accentuates the parapet and cornice.

Corner of Kanawha Blvd. and Capitol Streets.

Union Building

Clarence L. Harding, architect. The tallest building in West Virginia at the time of its construction in 1911, the landmark Union Building is a symbol of Charleston's early banking and business concerns. It was originally named the Alderson-Stephenson Building in honor of businessmen Charles Alderson and Samuel Stephenson, the men who financed its construction. Located at 723 Kanawha Blvd., East.

Victorian Block, Capitol Street

This group of buildings includes some of the oldest structures on Capitol Street, dating back to 1887.

Situated on the east side of Capitol Street between Virginia & Quarrier Streets

Virgil A. Lewis House

This was once the home of Virgil A. Lewis, West Virginia's first state historian and author of the book The Life and Times of Ann Bailey. The property was purchased in order to preserve his home and to provide an excellent site for a library building for the town of Mason. Located in Mason, West Virginia, is registered on the National Register of Historic Places. For information, phone 304-773-5200

Kincaid House

Located in Point Pleasant, this structure is an imposing three story brick house that was built between 1890 and 1900. The house is open for tours by appointment. Please contact Charles Humphreys at (304) 675-3844 for more information.

Museums and Collections

African-American Heritage Family Tree Museum

A private collection of photographs, household items, personal possessions; remembrances of John Henry and other famous African American West Virginians. Located in Ansted, West Virginia. 304-658-5526 Open to the public

Beckley Exhibition Coal Mine

This is a chance to visit an authentic coal mine; take a ride on a "man trip" car that will guide you through 1,500 feet of restored underground passages. You'll learn all about mining low seam coal, from the very first manual stages to modern mechanized operation. Beckley Exhibition Coal Mine is listed on the National Register of Historic Sites.

While you're there, be sure to visit the gift shop, coal company house and the superintendent's house. Be sure to bring a jacket! The temperature is a constant 58 degrees inside the mine.

Located about an hour's drive from Charleston on I-77S at exit 44. To get there, take the exit then turn East on Route 3 (Harper Rd.). Turn left on Ewart Ave. Go 1 mile to the New River Park entrance. Season is from April 1 to November 1. For more information phone (304) 256-1747 or visit http://www.beckleymine.com/

Blenko Glass

Discover the ancient art of glass blowing and find yourself surrounded by beauty and fine workmanship at Blenko Glass. Blenko Glass has created works for many famous buildings and museums. Decorative glassware is on display in the visitors' center and is available for purchase in the factory outlet display area. Blenko's museum features a designer's corner and an artistry exhibit. Observation deck tours are available to watch craftsmen at work.

Located approximately 40 minutes from Charleston on Route I-64 W in Milton, WV. For more information call (304) 743-9081 or visit www.blenkoglass.com

Ceredo Caboose Museum and History Row

History Row in the center of the city celebrates railroad history. Look for historical artifacts and railroad memorabilia in the restored "caboose museum" and see the best preserved petroglyph in the country: a 77" Indian Petroglyph which bears the image of the ancient "Water Monster's Daughter". There's also a collection of 50-year-old handblown glass and a historical archives. For more information call 304-453-3025.

Coal Heritage Museum

Downtown museum showcasing coal heritage and memorabilia. Located at 347 Main St. in Madison. For more information please phone 304-369-5180 or visit www.wvcoalmuseum.org

Coal Heritage Trail

A national scenic byway that travels through Wyoming Fayette Raleigh McDowell and Mercer counties. The coal heritage trail is one of only 22 designated national heritage areas in the country. For more information call 304-256-6941 or visit www.coalheritage.org .

Coal Miner's Statue

This statue stands on the lawn of the Boone County Courthouse and was created as a tribute to all coal miners. It was erected in the coal capital of West Virginia, where coal was discovered in 1742. The statue stands 7-feet 2-inches tall and is made from bronze and metal.while you're there, visit the Boone County Courthouse, which was started in 1914 and completed in 1921. The exterior is beautiful Indiana limestone and the edifice is on the National Register of Historic Places. For more information call 304-369-7301 or visit www.boonecountywv.org

Fenton Glass

Fenton is the largest manufacturer of handmade colored glass in the country. Visit the Fenton Glass museum that features glass made from 1907 to 1980, including the famous Carnival glass, or find first-quality, hard-to-find and retired pieces in the gift shop. Regularly scheduled tours allow visitors to watch craftsmen create their art.

Fenton Art Glass is located about an hour and a half's drive away in Williamstown, just off I-77N near Parkersburg. For more information call (304) 375-7772 or (800) 319-7793. Visit Fenton online at www.fentongiftshop.com

Historic Matewan, WV

Matewan was the site of the "Battle of Matewan", a significant labor dispute caused by coal company executives who were trying to evict union workers from company housing. The gunfight at Matewan left 10 dead and several wounded. It led to the eventual end of coal companies' control over the workers in West Virginia.

The town of Matewan is listed as a National Historic Landmark. It offers visitors a Matewan Depot replica, live re-enactments, and walking tour of the Historic District. For information phone 304-426-4239 or visit www.matewan.com

Huntington Museum of Art

West Virginia's largest fine art museum. Both public and private collections from around the region bring together artistic trends, varied media, juried exhibitions, and works from some of the top artists in the country.

2033 McCoy Rd., Huntington. Visit www.hmoa.org

Huntington Railroad Museum

Located at Memorial Boulevard and 14th Street West, in Huntington's Ritter Park, this outdoor museum features a variety of train equipment and cars on display.

The museum is open free every Sunday from 2-5 P.M., between Memorial Day and September 30th.

Jenkins Plantation Museum

A large brick house built in 1835, this was the home of Confederate General Albert Gallatin Jenkins. The home originally stood on 4,000 acres. IT stands on the banks of the Ohio River and is listed on the National Register of Historic Places. Hours: Tuesday through Saturday, 10 a.m. to 4 p.m. Closed Sunday and Monday. Located on West Virginia Route 2 approximately 15 miles north of Huntington at 8814 Ohio Rd. Lesage. For more information phone 304-762-1059

Mothman Museum and Research Center

This museum is dedicated to an archive that contains information about various Mothman sightings over the years. The museum features all sorts of rare collectables, as well as movie props from the "Mothman Prophecies" movie starring Richard Gere. A visual media viewing area, gift shop, and free local information can also be found at this museum. Located in the heart of Point Pleasant's historic downtown. For more information visit http://www.mothmanmuseum.com/index.html

Museum in the Park

Regional cutural center located at Chief Logan State Park. The exhibits of local and regional history and arts and crafts change seasonally. For more information call 304-792-7229

Salt Worker's Heritage Park

This fenced compound contains elements that were common to the early salt worker's life. Visitors will find a reproduction of Booker T. Washington's cabin, a school building, children's museum, storage shed, animal pens, and a period garden. Located at 2404 Malden Drive, Malden.

The park is open for tours by arrangement. Tours take approximately one hour and admission is $1 for children, $2 for adults. Phone 304-925-9499

The Museum in the Community

Originally started as collaboration between the Huntington Museum of Art and some high Scholl students, the former strip mall Museum has expanded to become a true exhibition, arts education center, and cultural center for visitors of all ages. The Museum has had over 100 exhibits and 75 performances. The summer arts camp features visual arts, dance, music, and drama. Located at 3 Valley Park Drive in Hurricane. Phone 304-562-0484 or visit www.museuminthecommunity.org

The Museum of Radio and Technology, Inc.

This is the biggest museum of radios, televisions and electronic equipment in the USA, including a circa 1920s radio sales, repair and parts store. See a priceless collection of technology dating back to the invention of the radio. Stroll through a broadcasting studio and view the fully operational amateur "ham" radio station, which is on the air and available for use by those visitors who carry a valid FCC amateur radio license. Located at 1640 Florence Ave., Huntington

Free admission. Hours: 10am to 4pm (Sat) and 1-4 pm (Sun) all year. 10am to 4pm (Fri) in the summer. For information, call 304-525-8890 or see http://zip.to/mrt

West Virginia State Farm Museum

Dedicated to the preservation of Mason County's agricultural heritage, this museum is home to hundreds of antiques from tools to tractors. The museum is also the site of dozens of historic buildings which have been moved from their original locations, rebuilt and preserved. http://www.wvfarmmuseum.org/

West Virginia Veterans Memorial Plaza

A two-story monument on State Capitol grounds. Four monoliths dedicated to World War I and II, Korea and Vietnam display names of the war dead within the sanctuary of the classically styled Memorial. Ramped walkways over the oval reflecting pool affords easy access to the sanctuary display of some 10,000 names. 304/558-0230.

Motor Sports and Racing

Beckley Motor Speedway

3/8 mile, high banked clay oval track. Late Models, Semi-Lates, AMRA Modifieds, Street Stocks, 4-cylinder stocks.

I-77 to exit 48, then 1.5 miles east, then .7 miles south on US 19, then.5 miles west, then .5 miles north.

Racing every Saturday night. For more information call 304-877-5581 or visit www.beckleymotorspeedway.com

Benjy's Motorcycle Museum

Harley-Davidson motorcycle museum with 10000 square feet of motocycles from 1909 to present.

408 4th St., Huntington

Benjy's Harley-Davidson

Harley-Davidson retail store with 50s style diner; motorcycle museum and Motorclothes apparel. 304-523-1340. www.benjyshd.com

Catfish Speedway

www.catfishraceway.com

304-743-5400 or 304-697-0842

300' Dirt Drag Strip and Demolition Derby Pit.

I-64 to exit 8. Go South on Rt. 152 to Wayne. Track is approx. 1 mile south of Wayne on the left. 5148 Lowr Newcomb Creek Road, Huntington, WV 25704

Racing every Saturday night

I-77 Speedway

304-372-5328

3/8 mile, semi-banked dirt oval track. Late models, Semi-lates, Modifieds, Street Stocks and Four-Cylinder Stocks.

1-77 to exit 132, then .1 mile east on SR 21, then .3 mile south on Cedar Lakes Road, then .3 mile.

Racing every Saturday night

Kanawha Valley MotorSports Park

http://www.kanrace.com/

West Virginia's only IHRA sanctioned raceway.

I-64 Winfield Exit #39. North on Rt 34 to Rt 35 North. 15 miles to track.

Ona Speedway

7/16 mile, semi-banked, asphalt oval track. Special events track.

I-64 to exit 20-A, then .2 mile south, then 2.8 miles east on SR 60. 2.6 miles north on Howell Mills Rd., then bear right and go 1.1 miles and ease on Prichard Rd. Behind airport.

Special Events only. Phone 304-743-4523 or visit www.onaspeedway.com

Tri-State Racetrack and Gaming Center

Greyhound Dog Racing, Simulcast dog and horse racing over 90,000 square feet of gaming enteraintment and 1800 slot machines. Take I64 west 11.1 miles to WV-

622/Goff Mtn Road exit -Exit 47 towards Cross Lanes, turn left onto WV-622/Goff Mountain Rd Straight 08 miles on Lakeview Dr to the track 304-776-1100 www.tristateracetrack.com

Tyler Mountain Raceway

1/8 mile dirt oval Kart Racing Track. Stock Light, Stock Medium, Stock Heavy, Super Heavy, Tights, Purple, Blue, Gold, Yard Karts and Champ Karts.

I-64 to exit 50, Cross Lanes exit. Go north on Route 622 to Rocky Fork Rd., turn left on Rocky Fork for 1.2 miles. Turn left on Sandstone Dr. to the track.

Racing every Friday night. 304-776-2636

Golf

Berry Hills Country Club

www.berryhillscc.com 18-hole private golf course. One Berry Hills Rd., Charleston WV 25314 phone 304-744-8790

Big Bend Golf Club

18 holes, par 71, 6,044 yards;
Riverview Dr., Torando
304-722-0400
www.kcprc.com

Edgewood Country Club
18 hole private golf course

304-984-9207
www.edgewoodcc.com

Esquire Country Club
18-hole public golf course.
One Esquire Rd., Barboursville, WV
304-736-1476

18 holes, par 55, 2,240 yards;
2000 Coonskin Drive, Charleston
304/341-8013.
www.kcprc.com

Little Creek Golf Course
304-746-GOLF
99 Fairway Dr., South Charleston

Logan Country Club
304-855-9018
18-hole public golf course.
Rt 10, Chapmanville, WV 25508.

Meadowland Golf Course
888-GOLF-521
9-hole public golf course.
Rte 35, Winfield, WV

Riverview Country Club
304-369-9835
18-hole public golf course.
Rt 17, Riverview Course, Danville, WV 25053

Sandy Brae Golf Course
www.kcprc.com
304-965-6800
18 holes, par 69, 5,876 yards;
19 Osborne Mills Rd., Charleston. (Amma Exit, 1-79)

Scarlet Oaks Country Club
304/755-8079.
18 holes, par 72, 6,021 yards; semi-private
#1 Dairy Rd., Poca

Shawnee Golf Course
304-341-8030
9 holes, par 72, 5,956 yards;
Shawnee Regional Park Route 25, Institute

Sleepy Hollow Golf Club
304-757-6581
18-hole private golf course.
3780 Sleepy Hollow Rd., Hurricane, WV

Shopping

Bridge Road Shops

Creative and distinctive shopping; Shops specialize in selected items for home decorating, accessories, gifts, clothing and more. Located on Bridge Road, close to downtown Charleston. Phone 304-342-6972

Capitol Market

A renovated train frieght station from the 1800s. An indoor and outdoor market offering specialty shops inside and farmer's market located outside with seasonal items available year round.

Located at 800 Smith St. in downtown Charleston. 304/344-1905. www.capitolmarket.net

Charleston Town Center Mall

One of the nation's largest downtown enclosed shopping malls, featuring 130 specialty stores, three major department stores, Picnic Place and specialty restaurants. The Center Court Atrium with its three-story waterfall and extensive greenery is a favorite with visitors and locals alike. Adjacent to Charleston Civic Center at Clendenin, Court, Lee and Quarrier Streets. 304/345-9525. www.charlestontowncenter.com

Dudley Farms Plaza

Shops include Kohl's, Goody's, Books-A-Million, Michaels, and several others.

Located at Highway 119S and Green Road, South Charleston.

Kanawha Coin & Relics

Coins & currency, small collectibles and antiques.

v712 Fife St., Charleston, WV 25301. Open Mon-Fri 9:30 a.m. - 5 p.m. and Sat 9:30 a.m. - 3 p.m. Phone 304-342-8081

Kanawha Mall

304/925-4921.
Convenient one level shopping with 40 stores and eateries, including Elder-Beerman, Gabriel Brothers and Waldenbooks.

Located at 57th St. and MacCorkle Ave., SE, Kanawha City, Ten minutes from downtown Charleston.

Milton Flea Market

Flea market offering a variety of goods.
I-64 Exit 28; Milton.
Phone 304-743-1123 or visit the website at www.miltonfleamarket.com

Nitro Antique Mall

304/755-5002

More than 31 vendors with 3 floors of antiques, furniture and collectibles!

110 21st St., Nitro, WV 25143.

Riverwalk Plaza

T.J. Maxx, S&K Menswear, Blockbuster Video in addition to many other shops and eateries.

Located on MacCorkle Avenue, SW, in South Charleston.

Somewhere in Time Antiques

Find just about anything you're looking for! With more than 55 vendors carrying various eras of antiques & collectibles.

307 21st St., Nitro, WV 25143.

Mon-Sat 10 a.m. - 6 p.m.; until 8 p.m. on Thursday and Sun 10 a.m. - 5 p.m.

South Charleston Antique Mall
304-744-8975
Open 7 days a week
6167 D St., South Charleston, WV 25303.

Mon, Tues, Wed, Fri, & Sat 10 a.m. - 5 p.m., Thur 10 a.m.- 8 p.m. & Sun 12 p.m. -4 p.m.

Southridge Centre

Stores include Wal-Mart, Sam's Wholesale Club, Fashion Bug and many more.

Located on Corridor G (Rt. 119s), South Charleston.

Tamarack

http://www.tamarackwv.com/

800-225-5982

Shop in the largest collection of quality West Virginia crafts, art, gourmet foods, books and recordings.

This eight-story office building was originally the National City Bank. Fine cream-colored terra cotta trim decorates the parapet and cornice.

Exit 45, off I-77, Beckley. 1-88-TAMARACK.

Visions Day Spa

304-345-5620

Salon and day spa; hair; nails; licensed massage therapy; makeovers.

238 Capitol Street Charleston

Sports Facilities and Coliseums

Cam Henderson Center

http://www.marshall.edu/

(304) 696-5275.

Home of Marshall University Thundering Herd Basketball. Complete multi-purpose physical education facility with adjacent track and field.

Charleston Civic Center and Coliseum

http://www.charlestonwvciviccenter.com/

304/345-7469

Year-round entertainment, convention, exhibition and sporting events. Top rock, country, gospel and Broadway acts, circus, hot rod pull, wrestling, home show and sports show. The Civic Center Coliseum is a 13,500-seat showplace for concerts, and a 12,500 seat arena for basketball.

Civic Center Dr. Charleston

University of Charleston's Laidley Field

304/348-1134.

Laidley's stadium, football, soccer and track facility, has one of the finest metric tracks in the eastern United States and seats 18,600. Regularly scheduled annual events include West Virginia High School Track and Field Championship in May, State High School North-South All-Star Football game in June and the Kanawha County High School Majorette Festival in September. Outdoor concerts and Ribfest also are featured during the summer months.

Located in Charleston's East End near the Capitol Complex.

West Virginia Power

http://www.wvpower.com/

304-344-CATS.

With more than 70 home games a season, the Class "A" minor league affiliates of the Milwaukee Brewers—a Major League Baseball franchise—offers up plenty of action with clutch hits, strikeout pitching, and plenty of fun with fireworks, giveaways and special promotions that are sure to be a home run with the enitre family. And bring the kids to see the Power Pack! Catch a game from April through September at beautiful Appalachian Power Park, Charleston's new $23 million dollar stadium in the heart of downtown.

Take 1-64 east to exit 100. Turn left at 2nd light onto Lee St., turn left at 2nd light onto Morris St. Go through 2 lights. The park is on the left.

See website for schedule.

West Virginia Wild Basketball

An International Basketball League team based in Charleston, the WVW was begun in 2005 as an exhibition team and started their se son in earnest with the 2006 schedule. 717 Lee Street East Suite 301 Charleston, WV 25302

Tel: (304) 720-2244 Fax: (304) 720-2245

Cultural Entertainment

Capitol Center Theatre

From the day it opened in 1914 as a vaudeville showplace, to its later transformation as a movie theatre, the West Virginia Capitol Theatre has starred as one of Charleston's leading entertainment attractions. It was restored and reopened as the Capitol Center in 1984. This magnificent historical landmark continues to provide a wide variety of entertainment as part of

West Virginia State University. Located at 123 Summers Street.

Charleston Ballet (American Academy of Ballet)

www.thecharlestonballet.com

304-342-6541

This civic troupe has enriched the cultural life of WV performing traditional and original ballets.

Charleston Chamber Music Society

www.charlestonchambermusic.org

304-344-5389

The Society's 65th year of presenting classical chamer music concerts.

Charleston Light Opera Guild

www.charlestonlightoperaguild.org

304-342-9312

West Virginia's premier producer of community musical theater.

Charleston Stage Company

http://www.charlestonstagecompany.com/

304-343-5772

This multicultural theatre company performs theatre productions for West Virginia audiences. For more than a decade, Charleston Stage Company has been doing experimental, avant garde plays, new drama and European and American classic dramas.

Clay Center for the Arts & Sciences

http://www.theclaycenter.org/

304/561-3500.

Considered one of the most ambitious cultural and educational undertakings in West Virginia, the Clay Center was established to serve the arts, science, and technology by bringing together performances in dance, music and theater, and educational programming and exhibits. This state-of-the-art facility includes Clark Performance Place, which includes the Maier Foundation Performance Hall, a 1,880-seat world-class theater, as well as the versatile Walker Theater. The Clay Center is also home to the Avampato Discovery Museum and the West Virginia Symphony Orchestra. Festival delle Arti outdoor bronze sculpture

One Clay Sq. Charleston

Chuck Mathena Center for the Performing Arts

www.thechuckmathenacenter.com

304-425-5128

Professional artists; quality entertainment; educational opportunities. Scheduled to open March 2007.

Stafford Dr. Princeton

Historic LaBelle Theater

www.southcharlestonwv.org

800-238-9488

All exhibitions programming and operations take place inside the historic LaBele Theater.

311 D St. South Charleston

Kanawha Players Official State Theatre of WV

www.www.kanawhaplayers.org

304-343-7529

Community theater group offering live productions.

Mountain Stage

http://www.mountainstage.org/

304/342-5757

West Virginia Public Radio's live two-hour arts performance show is hosted on Sundays at 6:00 pm at the Cultural Center Theater in the State Capitol Complex, with approximately 26 shows taped per year. The show features nationally and internationally recognized musicians. Mountain Stage is one of the most popular programs offered to Public Radio International's member stations and is heard on 130 PRI stations nationwide.

Mountaineer Opry House

The Mountaineer Opry House in Milton, WV, is the local hot spot for traditional Bluegrass Music in a family-friendly setting. Shows are held most Saturday nights at 7:30 p.m. Located at the Milton exit of I-64 10 minutes east of Huntington or 20 minutes west of Charleston.

West Virginia Symphony Orchestra

www.wvsymphony.org

304/342-0160.

Season runs from September through April with a schedule of symphonic and pop performances. The Orchestra also presents Symphony Sunday in June.

The Mountain State New River Gorge Mystery Train

www.themysterytrain.com

866-529-6412

Live Audience Participation, Professional Mystery Theater & Regional Musical Entertainment On Selected Rail Tours.

West Virginia Archives and History Library

www.wvculture.org

304-558-023

Collects; preserves and provides public access to historical documents and records.

1900 Kanawha Blvd. E Bldg 9

West Virginia Cultural Center

304-431-4698

This magnificent Center houses exhibits in the State Museum and research materials in the Archives. The State Theatre features concerts, films, lectures, and theatrical presentations and Mountain Stage performances.

State Capitol Complex

The Cultural Center is open Monday through Thursday 9 am to 8 pm; Friday and Saturday 9 am to 6 pm; Sunday 12 to 6 pm. The West Virginia Archives is open Monday to Thursday 9 am to 8 pm; Friday and Saturday 9 am to 6 pm. Closed on state holidays. For tour reservations call 304/558-4839 or 1-800-CALL-WVA.

Civil War Sites

www.bluegraytrail.com

304-927-1780

Visit historic Civil War sites. Replica of log cabin. Remains of earthwork fortifications.

Off of Williams Dr.; Spencer

Class VI River Runners Inc.

http://www.raftwv.com/ or www.class-vi.com

304/574-0704 or 1-800-CLASS VI (252-7784)

America's best rafting on the New and Gauley rivers in West Virginia. High quality outfitting at a reasonable price for ages six to 86, 1/2 day to seven day trips available. Scenic float trips to Class V + whitewater. Experience one of North America's most scenic and culturally fascinating regions. Groups of two to 600 can be accommodated.

Parks

Danner Meadows Park

www.cityofcharleston.org

304-348-6860

A beautiful family park providing open athletic field, walking track, adult fitness stations, picnic shelter and playground.

Located in Fort Hill off South Fort Dr. and Longwood Rd.

Davis Park

A quiet oasis of greenery linking Capitol and Summers Streets. It features an equestrian statue of Henry G. Davis, U.S. Senator from West Virginia, 1871-83, railroader and vice presidential candidate. Davis is also honored with a copy of this statue in Elkins, West Virginia.

Capitol and Lee Streets.

Kanawha State Forest

www.wvstateparks.com

304/558-3500

A favorite for outdoor activities, everything from a small picnic to a full-fledged scouting weekend. 46 campsites offer a variety of ways to rough it. Other activities in this 9,300-acre forest include swimming, hiking, biking, hunting, fishing and year-round horseback riding.

I-64 Exit 58A, then US 119 South to Oakwood Road and follow the signs.

New River Gorge Bridge

The New River Gorge is wonderfully diverse and visually spectacular, hence its nickname "The Grand Canyon of the East". It is renowned for its excellent fishing, rock climbing and mountain biking opportunities, but it is best known for being the home of America's Best Whitewater. The New River Gorge Bridge is one of the world's largest single-arch steel span bridge. New River Gorge National River Visitor Center

Oakmont Park

Little league ball field, picnic area, basketball court and playground.

Oakmont and Spruce Rds in South Hills

Ritter Park Tennis Center

www.huntingtontennis.com

304-696-5977

Eleven hard courts situated in a natural setting. In winter four courts are covered with a bubble.

1571 Ritter Park Dr. Huntington

Sunset Park

A small cozy park offering a basketball court, picnic shelter and playground.

Capitol Hill

Activities and Adventures

Drift-A-Bit Whitewater Rafting

304/574-3282 or 1-800-633-7238.

Affordable whitewater rafting on the New and Gauley rivers - from family adventure to adrenaline-packed excitement. For information, write to P.O. Box 885, Fayetteville, WV 25840.

Foxfire Hot-Air Balloon Rides

www.foxfirewv.com

Hot Air Balloon rides (reservation required)

US Rt 60 Milton, WV, only 12 miles East of Huntington

Hurricane Skate Park

304-562-5896.

Skateboarding and in-line skating have become a popular sport for all ages. Hurricane has taken positive action to provide a safe environment for this new pastime. Skateboarding equipment including ramps, quarter pipes, half pipes and a fun box provide challenges for young and old alike. The Skate Park is located within Hurricane City Park and is open during park hours for the public. Safety helmets and pads are strongly advised and required for planned events.

Scary Creek Paintball

(304) 755-5973 or (800) 870-5973.

A fun way to spend a day with friends at the tri-state's largest paintball field. Scary Creek has five houses, forts, streams, foxholes that can be incorporated in a game. Also enjoy the snack bar and indoor/outdoor picnic area. Restrooms and showers also available.\

Located about 35 minutes from Charleston off I-64W.

Open daily June-Labor Day. Open weekends from September-May.

South Charleston Memorial Ice Arena

www.scmemorialicearena.com

304-744-ICE

Year-round ice skating, which includes daily public sessions, learn to skate program, plus a heated viewing area. Individual and family passes.

Shops of Trace Fork (off Rt. 119).

Southridge Grand Prix Family Fun Center

www.southridgegrandprix.com

304-720-4FUN

Indoor kart racing, lazer tag, 3 indoor tracks, video game arcade and racing leagues. Private party rooms.

500 Southridge Blvd. Charleston, WV (next to the movie theater)

SUMMER - 12pm to 11pm S-Th, 10am to 12am F-Sat FALL - 3pm to 10pm M-Th, 3pm to 12am F, 10am to 12am Sat, 12pm to 9pm Sun

USA Raft

800-USA-RAFT

Express whitewater rafting on the New and Gauley rivers. Our express trips have all the excitement of a full day trip in about half the time and at a reasonable cost. New River express at 9:30 am and 2:30 pm, March through November. Gauley express Friday through Monday in September and October. Call for dates and times. Rt. 3, Box 430, Fayetteville, WV 25840.

Rural Rte 3 Fayetteville

Venture Lanes

304-768-7307

Thirty-two lanes of bowling; bar and grill; meeting room

6300 MacCorkle Ave. St. Albans

Wildwater Expeditions

www.wvaraft.com

Wine Cellars

Dunbar Wine Cellar

304-766-0223

Picnic shelter; fishing; nature walk and archery range.

Dutch Hollow Wine Cellars Park

304/766-0223.

Last known remnants of a once thriving industry built around 1855. One of only two such wine cellars east of the Mississippi River. Dunbar Exit off I-64, follow State Route 25 to the park. Contact Rod Harless,

Roane Vineyards

www.roanevineyards.com

877-927-WINE

Farm winery; tasting room; sales and tours. Seasonal events.

1585 Reedyville Rd. Spencer

For children

Appalachian Children's Choir

www.wvacc.org

304/343-1111.

This is a community based audition-tuition children's choral program consisting of five choirs for children, grades Kindergarten through twelve. The Appalachian Children's Choir performances include a variety of music. The annual concert season includes two holiday concerts in December, a Benefit Concert in February, and two spring concerts—one in April and May.

Appalachian Power Park

304-344-2287

Home stadium of the West Virginia Power. Also the site of special high school and university baseball tournaments as well as concerts in the summer.

601 Morris St. Charleston

Avampato Discovery Museum

http://www.avampatodiscoverymuseum.org/

304/561-3575.

Located inside the Clay Center for the Arts and Sciences-WV, the Avampato Discovery Museum features two floors of interactive science exhibits, a world class art museum, and the ElectricSky (TM) Theater showing large format films, laser shows and planetarium shows.

Museum galleries are open Wednesday thru Saturday 10am to 5pm and Sunday 12pm to 5pm. Call for ElectricSky (TM) Theater show titles and times.

Capitol Nannies

info@capitolnannies.com

304-757-1298

Full-time nanny service with temporary sitting available for hotel guests.

Children's Theatre of Charleston

www.ctoc.org

304-346-0164

Since 1932 the Children's Theatre of Charleston has educated children about the theater.

WaterWays Waterpark

www.waterwayspark.com

304-369-6125

Slides; Pool; kiddie pool; go-karts; mini-golf; archery range; walking trail and picnic shelters.

US 119; Julian

Waves of Fun

304-562-0518

Water park, Mini-golf and Sand Volleyball

I-64, exit 34 - Hurricane, Valley Park Dr.

Memorial Day to Labor Day

Educational Opportunities

University of Charleston -2300 MacCorkle Ave SE Charleston WV Full-time enrollment: 1,200. http://www.ucwv.edu 1-800-995-GOUC

WEST VIRGINIA STATE COLLEGE - about 12 miles away 5000 Fairlawn Ave., INSTITUTE, WV Full-time enrollment: 3,688. Www.wvstate.edu 304-766-3000

MARSHALL UNIVERSITY -about 51 miles away for the main campus, but with graduate studies in Charleston; One John Marshall Drive, HUNTINGTON, WV; Full-time enrollment: 12,361 http://www.marshall.edu. Phone 1-800-642-3463

WEST VIRGINIA UNIVERSITY AT PARKERSBURG -about 64 miles away 300 Campus Dr, PARKERSBURG, WV; Full-time enrollment: 2,306 Phone 304-424-8000 www.wvup.edu

OHIO UNIVERSITY-MAIN CAMPUS is located about 72 miles away; ATHENS, OH; Full-time enrollment: 18,721. Phone 740-593-1000 www.ohio.edu

CONCORD COLLEGE - about 80 miles away in ATHENS, WV; Full-time enrollment: 2,723. Phone 1-800-344-6679. www.concord.edu

BLUEFIELD STATE COLLEGE –located about 82 miles away in BLUEFIELD, WV; Full-time enrollment: 2,096. phone 304-327-4000/ www/bluefield.wvnet.edu/

HOCKING TECHNICAL COLLEGE – located about 84 miles away at 3301 Hocking Parkway, NELSONVILLE, OH; Full-time enrollment: 4,050. Phone 877-462-5464. www.hocking.edu.

Discover Charleston West Virginia

www.DiscoverCharlestonWV.com

Brought to you through the cooperation of these Charleston, WV businesses.

CPSIA information can be obtained at www.ICGtesting.com
Printed in the USA
BVOW010450121011

273437BV00001B/277/A